JONNY MURPHY @the_hungryhooker's

BAKES

and wee treats

EBURY
PRESS

Contents

Hello!

Thank you so much for buying my cookbook! You have no idea how grateful I am for the support. My name's Jonny, but many know me as The Hungry Hooker. I'm a former professional rugby player, who played the position of hooker until I had to retire early due to injury. I have always had a love for baking and it was this love that led to this moment, creating my own cookbook filled with my family's favourite Northern Irish recipes.

Baking was always a staple in our family, from my Nanny Mamie to my mum Wendy. My nanny and Granda Alfie looked after my wee sister and I during school holidays. If I wasn't pottering around in the garage with my granda, I was in the kitchen helping my nanny, making homemade jam, traditional breads and sweet treats. Back then, I was the chief taste tester before Granda stole my crown. Little did I know that the skills I learned then would follow me through life.

I've always baked – whether it was snacks for my teammates or for charity coffee mornings. I made treats once or twice a week for tough training days. A little bit of morale for the boys, to combat the wet and windy weather in the west. I started a wee Instagram page to post new bakes and ideas. I even started supplying some bakes now and then to the local coffee shops of Galway. But rugby was my life. I intended to play the game I loved until the wheels fell off. Yet after pouring 25 years of my life into that dream all it took was one phone call and it was over. I had to retire on medical grounds. The following day, I had a panic attack. I've always struggled with my mental health and I'm not ashamed to speak about it. If it helps lighten the burden of those struggling, it's worthwhile. Never be afraid to reach out for help – it's not weakness but a show of strength. And sometimes, it's the darker days that shape us into what we are today.

After the initial shock, I threw myself into the next chapter – a little wholesale bakery in the heart of Galway. All of my teammates from Connacht, my family, friends and loved ones encouraged me to give it a go. And for a time I supplied numerous coffee shops around Galway. Unfortunately, during this time my uncle Nigel passed away – my nanny's son. This was a tough time for everyone, but mostly for my grandparents. I felt a turning point came when months later they visited me in Galway for a break. I asked my nanny if she would show me her soda and potato farl recipes when I was next home. I started asking what we were making every time I visited. Eventually, Nanny was calling me asking the same when I was due back. In an unintentional way, baking had become therapy for us both. It was as if we had stepped back in time to when she looked after me as a child and we baked together.

Not long after, I made the decision to move back home and try to set up a bakery there. I started making easy-to-follow recipe videos to get more recognition online and help me sell more buns. And everything snowballed from there!

You won't find any complicated or difficult-to-find ingredients in this book. And you won't need any fancy equipment. I'm passionate about keeping things simple and knowing that what's in my food is simple too.

I also want you to remember that not everything has to be perfect. Baking is all about enjoying the process and the taste – a bit like life. Now don't get me wrong, if the recipe says to use eggs, please use eggs. Just don't put pressure on yourself to have it looking like a masterpiece. If it tastes good and you haven't burnt it, you're 99 per cent of the way there.

If this journey has taught me anything, it's that getting caught up in this mad world can take us away from what's really important in our lives: our family, our friends and those we love! Always strive to do what makes you happy with the people you love. If that's baking with your nanny, hanging out with your granda, working 9–5 or travelling the world, do it. I'm not ashamed to say I love baking and I love my grandparents. The fact that I can celebrate my family and their recipes in this book is a blessing and I will hold onto it forever. I hope you enjoy making these wee treats as much as we do!

Jonny x

Ingredients

I want this book to be accessible to everyone and that begins with the ingredients. If you have butter, flour, sugar, eggs and milk to hand you can make quite a lot of things. In my eyes, these are the essentials. As you go along, you'll slowly build up the other wee bits and pieces you need for your favourite bakes. I've used nothing you can't find in a good supermarket but here's a few notes on some of the slightly less common ingredients:

- I always use real pure salted butter in all my recipes (unless I've said otherwise). My go-to is Irish Kerrygold, but a good-quality brand will always see you right.
- Soda bread flour can be bought in most supermarkets, but you can make your own with 1 tsp bicarbonate of soda mixed into 450g plain flour.
- You can buy buttermilk in most supermarkets and it's best to use the real thing. If not available, for every 250ml milk stir in 1 tbsp lemon juice. Allow the mixture to stand for 10 minutes before using.

Essential Equipment

I'm not one for fancy equipment either. I try to keep things simple. But there are a few things you'll definitely need to make these recipes successfully.

- Weighing scales
- Set of measuring spoons (¼ teaspoon/ ½ teaspoon/5ml teaspoon/15ml tablespoon)
- Wooden spoon
- Whisk
- Silicone spatula
- Skewer (for testing cakes)
- A good sharp knife for slicing
- Pastry cutters (or you can always use a simple drinking glass)
- Rolling pin (or you can use a wine bottle – I've been known to use a bottle of Buckfast)
- Palette knife (optional, but handy for spreading icing)
- Fine-mesh sieve
- Kitchen scissors
- Loaf tins (I use both 450g/1lb and 900g/2lb tins)
- Cake tins (various sizes – I mostly use 20cm/8in and 23cm/9in tins)
- Springform tin (for making cheesecakes)
- Large mixing bowl
- Wire cooling rack
- Baking trays (various sizes)
- Handheld mixer/beaters (useful, but not essential)
- Stand mixer, with dough hook (optional)
- Food processor (useful, but not essential)
- Heatproof glass bowl (for melting chocolate – a bain-marie)
- Saucepans
- Frying pan
- Chopping board

Nanny Mamie's Top Baking Tips

- **Weigh everything out before you get stuck in,** as well as lining any tins. It just takes the stress out of it all and sets you up for success. As they say, 'fail to prepare, prepare to fail'.
- **If you don't have any greaseproof paper,** just grease your baking tin/tray and dust the inside with flour, tapping out the excess.
- **To line a round tin,** place it on your greaseproof paper, draw around the tin with a pencil and cut the circle out with scissors. Grease the tin with butter and place the circle of greaseproof in the tin, dusting the sides with some flour.
- **To line a loaf tin,** grease the whole tin with butter. Cut a long strip of greaseproof paper to the width of the tin and lay it up the middle lengthways. Throw in a wee bit of flour and shake this about until it lightly covers the sides and tap the excess out of the tin. Place a little bit of your cake mixture below each end of the greaseproof paper to stick it to the tin.
- **When mixing your ingredients,** scrape down the sides and bottom of your bowl halfway through. This ensures all your ingredients are fully combined.
- **When blind baking,** use baking beans. If you don't have any, you can use a packet of dried peas or uncooked rice. Keep them and reuse them for blind baking moving forward. Don't try to eat them!
- **When baking a wee loaf cake or something similar,** make a crease down the middle of your cake mixture with the back of a teaspoon before placing it in the oven. This will help it from rising too much in the middle and cracking.
- **When testing to see if your cakes are baked,** insert a skewer into the middle. If it comes out clean, your cake is baked and you won't go far wrong. All of our ovens differ and this is a trusty wee tip to help.
- **To prove dough,** a great place is inside on the windowsill in some sunlight. If it's too cold, flick your oven on for a few minutes until it's slightly warm when you stick your hand in, then turn it off and place your dough in the oven to prove. This will speed the process up during those colder months.
- **When making pastry,** make sure you have very cold ingredients (take your butter straight from the fridge and use ice-cold water).
- **When rolling out pastry,** place your baking tin, pie dish or dinner plate over the top to see if it's the correct size.

How to Knead Dough

Kneading bread dough can be a little daunting at first, but honestly there's nothing to fear. Obviously, the easiest way is to attach a dough hook to your stand mixer and allow it to do all the heavy work. But if you don't have one of these, you can do it the old-fashioned way, by rolling up your sleeves and using some elbow grease.

Lightly dust your work surface with some flour and pop your room-temperature dough onto it. Depending on the type of dough you're working with, things can get a little sticky and messy, but just trust the process. If it's too sticky to begin with, lightly dust the top of the dough with some extra flour. When working with very wet dough it can be tempting to add lots of extra flour, but be very light on this or use none at all. The more flour you add, the denser and tougher your bread will become. Be patient with your dough and keep working through the process below.

With the heel of your palm, push and stretch the dough away from you. Next, fold it back over the top towards you. I like to rotate it 90 degrees at this point and repeat the same pushing and folding back process. Depending on what the recipe method calls for, you will generally repeat this motion for about 5–10 minutes. The dough should be kneaded enough when your work surface and hands are fairly clean of any dough and flour, and the dough itself is smooth, soft, springy and elastic.

A few signs to know whether your dough is well kneaded are:

- IT WILL BE SMOOTH AND SHINY – When you've first mixed your dough, it can look lumpy. As you knead, it will become smooth.
- IT WILL BE TACKY – When kneaded, your dough will be silky smooth and tacky rather than sticky to the touch.
- IT WILL SPRING BACK – During the kneading process, press your finger into the dough. If the indentation mark remains visible, your dough requires more kneading and elbow grease.
- TRY THE WINDOWPANE TEST – Tear off a piece of dough and stretch it between your fingers. If your dough stretches without ripping, forming a translucent rectangle, you're good to go.

It's hard to overwork dough by hand as you tend to get the feel for it during the process. However, this can easily happen when using a machine, so keep a close eye on it. Over-kneading will result in a dense and easily tearable dough, which will produce a flat and dense loaf.

Now you can shape your dough into the desired shape and allow it to rise, following the individual recipe instructions.

How to Make the Perfect Cuppa Tae

I've never been one to toot my own horn, but I was told I needed to include my method on how to make the 'perfect' cup of tea in the book. My friends always harp on about it. When we were photographing the book, the shoot team lived on the many cups of tea I made. So here we are!

There's two ways to wet the cup – make a lovely big pot or a single mug. I'll tell you about both.

THE POT
I use an enamel or metal teapot for this job. Get your kettle boiling and gather 3 of your favourite tea bags. I like to give the pot a wee rinse and get a bit of heat in it to start, so once your kettle has boiled, pour a little into the teapot and swirl it around. Fire your tea bags into the pot and pour your boiling water in. I make sure to pour it directly onto the tea bags to get things going. Fill 'er up to just shy of the top, then get it onto your hob over a high heat. Allow it to come to a boil, keeping a close eye on it. Just before it boils, I like to get a teaspoon and press the tea bags against the side. I do this maybe 8–10 times and swirl them around the pot. Once it starts to boil, take the pot off the hob and onto a wee tea mat. Trust me, you don't want to burn your nanny's or mum's worktop. Now pour a wee jig into your mug to see if it's strong enough. We're all different, but I like a strong cup of tea, so I look for a nice dark colour. If it's not quite there, I'll give the bags a few more squeezes with the teaspoon and swirl it again, then it's good to go. Fill your mugs and then it's down to preference if you're having milk and sugar. We only take on the milk, because there's more than enough sweet stuff floating about our house, as you know!

THE MUG
Sometimes you don't need a full pot of tea. I use this method most of the time because I'm knocking back about 5 cups or more a day. Side note: I have a wide array of mugs and the one I use for a cup of tea solely comes down to my mood. I don't know if you're the same? Do I want a big one, a wee one, a wider one or maybe one that was a gift and reminds me of something nice. This is one of my wee quirks, but I know for a fact my Mum wishes I didn't do it, because there's a copious amount of different mugs used on the daily.

First off, pick your mug (mood dependent). Get the kettle boiling and pop your favourite tea bag into your mug. Depending on how much milk you like, fill it up leaving about an inch or so for milk. Now let it sit a' peace for about 90 seconds. Don't forget about it! My dad always shouts at me, saying, 'If you leave that tea bag in there any longer you'll be able to walk on it.' After taking some light abuse, take a teaspoon and press your tea bag into the side of your mug 3–4 times, then swirl it and repeat this twice more. Give your tea bag one last squeeze against the mug and get it out, adding your preferred amount of milk.

For me, the choice of milk has a big role to play in the finished article. I always say some whole milk really takes a cup of tea to the next level. It almost makes it creamy. If I could get my hands on the stuff fresh from the milk tank, like back in the day, I'd say it would be different gravy. This should make, in my eyes, the perfect single mug of tea, but we all have our opinions!

Who knew I could write so much about tea?

Loved by Alfie

My Granda Alfie is the chief taste tester in our house and he is some character. I got him to select his favourites from the book and you'll find them highlighted throughout with this stamp of approval, along with his wee comments.

Glossary of Northern Irish Slang

Here's some of the local words we use a lot in our family that'll make sure you fit right in if you ever visit.

A RAKE – A lot

A ROUND OF BREAD – Slice of bread

A WEE BUN – Any kind of sweet treat

AYE – A simple 'yes'

BANTER – Another way to describe great craic, a right laugh

CRAIC – Having fun, enjoyable, a good time

CRAIC'S NINETY – You know you're in for a good night

CULCHIE – Country person

CUPPA TAE – Cup of tea

DACENT FEED – Good hearty feed

DEADLY – Excellent, amazing, great

DIFFERENT GRAVY – So much better than anything else

EEJIT – Someone stupid or silly, who would make you laugh

BUCK EEJIT – Term of endearment for people who are silly

GET IT IN T' YE/KNOCK IT DOWN YE – Eat or drink it

GOOD GEAR – It's good stuff

GRAND – Great

HALLION – A good-for-nothing, can refer to a greedy person

PAN LOAF – Loaf of bread

POKE – Ice cream, generally one from an ice cream seller

QUARE – A lot, big, excellent, unusually, very (so many ways to use this one)

SIT A PEACE – Let it rest, leave it alone

SO IT IS – We're prone to sticking this phrase at the end of random sentences, no real meaning to it

SPUDS/MURPHY'S/TADDIES/BAGS OF FLOUR – Potatoes

TADDIE/TATTY BREAD – Potato bread

THAT'S A CRACKER – Good, great, funny

THAT'S FIERCE – Very, extremely

THAT'S MAGIC – Good, great

THAT'S PARFUL – Complimenting something

THAT'S SOME YOKE – It's nice

WET THE CUP/WET THE TEA – Make a cup of tea

WEE – This can be put in front of anything: 'a wee cup of tea', 'a wee bun'; or can just refer to something small

YARN – A wee chat

YE – You

YOKE – Can literally mean any item

Morning Treats

Crumpets

These are a classic breakfast treat, toasted with latherings of butter and your topping of choice. It might be hard to leave them until the next day, but if you do they develop a bit more texture. Either way, eating them fresh off the pan on a Sunday morning is hard to beat.

MAKES 6

150g plain flour
½ tsp salt
200ml lukewarm water, plus
 1 tbsp to activate the yeast
1 tsp instant dried (fast-action)
 yeast or active dry yeast
½ tsp caster sugar
1 tsp baking powder
2 tbsp butter, for greasing

1 Combine the flour, salt and 200ml lukewarm water in a bowl and whisk for about 2 minutes until smooth.

2 In a small separate bowl, combine the yeast with a tablespoon of lukewarm water and mix until dissolved.

3 Add the yeast mixture to the flour mixture, along with the sugar and baking powder, and whisk together until combined. Cover with a clean tea towel or some cling film and place in a warm place for 15–30 minutes until the surface is foamy. It won't increase that much in volume.

4 Grease some 9cm metal rings with butter – you can do several rings at a time depending on the size of your frying pan. Place them in the pan and set it over a medium–high heat. When you add your batter to the pan, it should sizzle gently; if it doesn't, the pan is not hot enough and this will result in no bubbles through your crumpets. Alternatively, if the pan is too hot, your crumpets will burn. Test by placing a little batter onto a butter knife and press it onto the pan. If it sizzles with no wisps of smoke coming out, it's good to go; if smoke emerges, reduce the heat under the pan.

5 Add 4 tablespoons of batter to each ring, about 1cm deep. Cook for 1½ minutes. Bubbles will start to appear on the surface but won't pop yet. Reduce the temperature slightly to medium and cook for a further minute. At this stage, some bubbles should begin to pop around the edges. Now reduce the heat to medium-low and cook for a further 2½–4 minutes until the surface is set. There should be no more bubbles popping at this point – if any are left, pop them with a skewer. Remove your rings (if necessary, run a knife around them to loosen), then flip each crumpet and cook the other side for 20–30 seconds just to colour.

6 Pop them onto a cooling rack, golden-side down, and leave to cool.

7 Repeat with the rest of the batter until all are cooked.

8 You eat these once cooled, but they are better the next day. Toast and lather in real butter and your favourite topping (I'm raspberry jam every time!).

Apple Pancakes

These are my spin on the apple pancakes I always got from the bakery as a young fella. I just find the apple to be a delicious addition to an already glorious treat. The thing I love so much about a pancake is it can fit into any time of the day. Breakfast – that's a given; a stack of them for brunch or lunch; a wee snack; or a light dinner or supper. I think it's easy to see I love a pancake, especially with a filling . . . and don't get me started on the toppings.

MAKES ABOUT 12

175g self-raising flour
1 tsp baking powder
175ml whole milk
1 egg, lightly beaten
45g soft light brown sugar
1–2 tsp ground cinnamon (optional)
1 large apple of choice (I prefer a green Granny Smith for its tartness), finely chopped or coarsely grated
butter, for frying

1 Sift the flour and baking powder into a bowl.

2 In a measuring jug, combine the milk, egg, sugar, cinnamon (if using). Mix well.

3 Create a well in the middle of your flour mixture and pour the milk mixture into this. Gradually mix with a fork, slowly incorporating a bit of the flour as you go. Mix until it's just smooth (over-mixing will make your pancakes tough). Gently stir in the apple until evenly distributed.

4 Heat a frying pan over a medium–low heat and add a knob of butter. This should sizzle nicely, but not burn. Spoon about 2 tablespoons of your pancake batter into the pan. (Depending on your pan, you can make more than one pancake at a time.) Cook until bubbles start to form and seem to set slightly – this should take around 2–3 minutes. Avoid increasing the heat to speed up the process – this will only result in you burning your pancakes and they won't cook through. When a fish slice or spatula slides effortlessly underneath, you're ready to flip. Flip your pancake and cook for around 1 minute more until golden.

5 You can serve these warm with some stewed apples or ice cream as a treat. Lemon curd is another great addition, or some fresh cream or Greek yogurt and honey. Alternatively, place them on a wire cooling rack and allow to cool fully, then enjoy as a quick lunch or snack on the go. They are delicious toasted and plastered in some real butter.

Boxty

If you're not from around my neck of the woods, it's hard to describe boxty. It's not quite potato bread or a pancake or even a hash brown – it's kind of a mixture of all three. But one thing's for certain – it's delicious. A great way to use up any leftover potatoes from the night before. I feel like it has to be a part of an Irish fry, but we all have our own slight differences when it comes to a fry up. Boxty is so versatile – I could eat it for breakfast, lunch and dinner, no problem.

MAKES 4–6

125g raw potato
125g cooked and mashed potato
75g plain flour
¼ tsp salt
½ tsp bicarbonate of soda
125ml buttermilk
knob of butter, for cooking

1 Grate the raw potato and squeeze out the excess moisture through a tea towel. Add to a mixing bowl along with the mashed potato and gently combine.

2 In a separate bowl, thoroughly combine the flour, salt and bicarbonate of soda, then add this to the potato mixture and mix well.

3 Gradually add the buttermilk, mixing between each addition. It will start to form a doughy sort of batter. Make sure it is well combined and no dry ingredients are left.

4 Heat a frying pan over a medium heat and add a good knob of butter to the pan. Once it is sizzling nicely, dollop heaped tablespoons of the potato mixture into the pan. Cook for about 3–5 minutes on each side until they form a nice crust and are cooked through.

5 Now plate up with the rest of your chosen breakfast items and tuck in. This is hearty food and great with any fry up.

English Breakfast Muffins

These are close to being my mum's and little sister's favourite breakfast snack. They're soft, chewy, and packed with flavour. All they need is a lathering of real butter after toasting. It will surprise you how much tastier these are than store-bought equivalents. When you realise how simple they are to make, you'll be having them every weekend morning.

MAKES 14

120ml water
180ml whole milk
2 tbsp caster sugar
7g (2¼ tsp) instant dried (fast-action) yeast
330g plain flour, plus extra for dusting
1 tsp salt
40g unsalted butter, melted
1 large egg, lightly beaten
vegetable oil, for greasing
semolina or cornmeal, for dusting

1 Combine the water, milk and sugar in a microwave-safe bowl and stir until dissolved. Gently heat the mixture in the microwave until lukewarm. Stir in the yeast and set aside for about 5 minutes, or until it develops a foamy top.

2 While the yeast activates, add the flour and salt to a large mixing bowl or stand mixer bowl and whisk together until combined.

3 Mix the melted butter and egg into the yeast mixture, then gradually pour this into the flour mixture while mixing with a spoon. If using a stand mixer, use a dough hook and mix on a medium-high speed for 6–8 minutes until the dough is smooth and elastic. If kneading by hand, knead on a lightly floured surface until smooth and elastic.

4 Pop the dough into a large, lightly oiled bowl, cover with a clean tea towel or some cling film and leave to rise in a warm place for about 1 hour, or until doubled in size.

5 Line 2 baking sheets with greaseproof paper and sprinkle with semolina or cornmeal. Turn the dough out onto a lightly floured surface and gently pat it out to about 2cm thick. With a floured 6cm round cutter, cut out your muffins and gently pop them onto the baking sheets. Re-roll any scraps and continue cutting out muffins until you've used up all the dough. Cover loosely with a clean tea towel or some cling film, and leave to prove in a warm place for about 30 minutes.

6 Heat a dry frying pan over a low heat. When you can feel the heat coming off the pan from a height of about 5cm, sprinkle it with semolina. Carefully add 3–4 muffins to the pan and cook for 5–6 minutes on each side. Transfer to a wire cooling rack. (If you find your muffins are still slightly underbaked in the middle, pop them into an oven preheated to 160°C fan/180°C/gas 4 for 3 minutes.) Clean the pan of semolina, then add a fresh sprinkle before cooking another batch of muffins. Allow them to cool if you have the patience, then slice in half, toast and slather in real butter.

Tea Loaf

If you're anything like me, ye love a cuppa tae, and what's better to go with it than a tea loaf? I'll admit when I was younger I didn't like the idea of this stuff. I thought fruit wasn't as good as chocolate. Boy, was I wrong. This, lathered in some real butter, will get you going. When I made this at home for the first time, my family went buck daft for it. You get a good wee feeling when someone enjoys your baking. I'm definitely a feeder and show my love by doing things for others, so when it was a hit I was special.

MAKES 1 LARGE LOAF

250g mixed fruit (sultanas, raisins, currants and cranberries)
40g glacé cherries, chopped
115g soft light brown sugar
250ml strong, hot black tea (I use 2 tea bags and let them wet for a good while)
1 egg, beaten
175g plain flour
1 tsp baking powder
1 tsp mixed spice
honey, for glazing

1 Combine the mixed fruit and glacé cherries in a bowl, along with the light brown sugar. Pour in the strong black tea and give it a good stir until all your sugar has dissolved. Cover with a clean tea towel and leave it to soak overnight – this will make your fruit nice and plump, giving a really moist and tasty loaf.

2 The next day, add the beaten egg and sift in the flour, baking powder and mixed spice. Mix this together with a fork or wooden spoon until it's fully combined.

3 Preheat the oven to 160°C fan/180°C/gas 4 and line a 900g (2lb) loaf tin with greaseproof paper.

4 Pour the batter into the prepared tin and flick the kettle on to make a cuppa tae while it's in the oven.

5 Bake for 1½ hours, or until a skewer inserted into the middle comes out clean. When you take it out, brush the top with honey and pop it back into the oven for another 5 minutes.

6 Allow it to cool for a few minutes in the tin and then transfer to a wire cooling rack to cool further. If you like it warm with butter drippin' down your chin, slice away, but be careful as it's so moist and delicate. If not, allow it to cool fully and then enjoy with a cuppa tae no doubt.

Cherry Scones

Scones will alway be a classic, especially for a late breakfast or lunch. This is my nanny's recipe and she has used it since she started baking herself, many years ago. I helped her make these all the time when I was younger and it's a treat being able to share them with you. You can have a batch of these rustled up in about 20 minutes, perfect for when you have a craving or want to treat guests. I love these fresh out of the oven, slightly warm, with real butter and homemade jam, but I'm sure you will have your own favourite toppings.

MAKES ABOUT 8

225g self-raising flour, plus extra for dusting
2 tsp baking powder
50g salted butter, softened and cubed
25g caster sugar
2 eggs
about 100ml buttermilk (or regular milk), as needed
100g glacé cherries, rinsed, dried and halved

1. Preheat the oven to 180°C fan/200°C/gas 6. Line a baking tray with greaseproof paper.
2. Sift the flour into a mixing bowl along with the baking powder. Add the softened butter to this and work it through using your fingertips. It will come together and form a nice crumb texture.
3. Sift in the caster sugar and mix thoroughly.
4. Crack 1 egg into a measuring jug and top up with buttermilk (or regular milk) until it reaches the 150ml mark. Gently beat these together.
5. Gradually add the buttermilk mixture to your dry ingredients, mixing with a fork between each addition, until a nice dough forms.
6. Dust the glacé cherries in a little flour, add them to the mix and fold them through.
7. Turn your dough out onto a lightly floured work surface and gently knead it, just enough to bring it together, then use a rolling pin to roll it out to about 2.5cm thick.
8. Cut your scones out with a floured 6cm pastry cutter or glass and place on your lined baking tray. Gather the scraps to form a last scone and place on the tray.
9. Beat the remaining egg for egg wash, then lightly brush the tops of the scones with it. Try to avoid letting the egg wash run down the sides of the scones.
10. Bake in the oven for about 12–15 minutes until they're a pale golden colour on top.
11. Remove from the oven and transfer to a wire cooling rack to let them cool down a little. These are best eaten fresh and I find them tastiest when slightly warm. You will be making these every week once you start, trust me!

Loved by Alfie

'Lovely with some real butter and jam, and a cuppa tae, of course!'

Cinnamon Swirl Banana Bread

Banana bread is good, but this cinnamon swirl banana bread is on another level. It locks in the moisture, caramelising throughout, giving a lovely crisp crust on top. What makes it even better is that you just chuck it all into one bowl and mix. I rustled this up for the first time when I was living in Galway. What I love about it though is that when I judged the Connacht Academy Bake Off, the winner later told me he had used this recipe. He was a man after my own heart!

MAKES 1 LARGE LOAF

225g salted butter, melted
200g caster sugar
1 tsp vanilla extract
2 large eggs
4 ripe bananas, mashed
240g plain flour
1 tsp bicarbonate of soda

For the cinnamon swirl
3 tbsp salted butter
3 tbsp caster sugar
3 tbsp soft dark brown sugar
2 tbsp ground cinnamon

1 Preheat the oven to 160°C fan/180°C/gas 4. Line a 900g (2lb) loaf tin with greaseproof paper.

2 Add the melted butter, caster sugar, vanilla extract and eggs to a large bowl. Whisk these together until they are combined and smooth, then add the mashed banana and mix this through. Sift in the flour and bicarbonate of soda, and gently fold through with a spatula until fully incorporated.

3 For the cinnamon swirl, melt the butter in a small pan or in the microwave in short 30-second bursts. Add both sugars to this along with the ground cinnamon and mix together with a spoon to form a sugary cinnamon paste.

4 Pour a quarter of the banana batter into your prepared tin and drizzle over a quarter of the cinnamon paste. Swirl this throughout with a skewer. Repeat this process until you have used up both of your mixtures.

5 Bake for about 1 hour–1 hour 10 minutes until golden on top and an inserted skewer comes out clean. If you feel like the top is browning too much, cover with some kitchen foil towards the end of the bake.

6 Allow to cool in the tin for about 30 minutes before removing to a wire cooling rack to cool fully. You can slice it slightly warm but it is very delicate. The kitchen will be smelling unreal after this and you will be drooling to get it sliced up.

Alfie's Blueberry Muffins

My Granda Alfie has a soft spot for a blueberry muffin. Don't ask me why, but the man just loves them. We tried out a few recipes on the well-known taste tester and these won hands down. They're lovely and soft, and packed with moist blueberries. You'll realise why he enjoyed them so much.

MAKES 12

- 225g plain flour, plus extra for dusting
- 175g caster sugar, plus extra for dusting
- 2 tsp baking powder
- 1 tsp salt
- 125g unsalted butter, melted and cooled
- 2 large eggs
- 125ml whole milk
- 1 tsp vanilla extract (optional)
- 300g blueberries

1. Preheat the oven to 170°C fan/190°C/gas 5. Pop 12 muffin cases into a muffin tin and set aside.
2. Sift the flour, sugar, baking powder and salt into a large mixing bowl. Whisk gently to combine, then set aside.
3. To a separate bowl, add the melted cooled butter, eggs, milk and vanilla (if using), whisking until combined and smooth.
4. Gradually add the wet ingredients to the dry ingredients, mixing together gently with a spatula.
5. Dust the blueberries in some flour, then add to your mixture and fold through.
6. Spoon the mixture evenly into the muffin cases and sprinkle the tops with some caster sugar. Bake for 30 minutes, or until golden brown on top and an inserted skewer comes out clean.
7. Remove from the oven and allow to cool in the tin for a few minutes before transferring to a wire cooling rack to cool fully. These are best eaten slightly warm and freshly baked with a lovely cup of coffee.

Loved by Alfie

'Can't get enough of them!'

Griddle Scones

A cross between a scone and a soda farl – a match made in heaven. Many people might not know what these are, but they're absolutely delicious. It's a shame that such great traditional recipes like this are slowly fading. They're getting harder and harder to find in local bakeries, so it was only right that these got a mention. Believe me, they deserve to be seen and more importantly eaten.

MAKES 8

225g plain flour, plus extra for dusting
1 tsp bicarbonate of soda
2 tsp cream of tartar
30g salted butter, cubed, plus extra for cooking
30g caster sugar
50g sultanas or raisins (optional)
about 150ml whole milk

1 Sift the flour, bicarbonate of soda and cream of tartar into a large bowl and lightly whisk to combine. Add the butter and rub in with your fingertips until the mixture resembles fine breadcrumbs.

2 Add the sugar and dried fruit (if using), stir through, then gradually add the milk, mixing with a fork to a soft, but not sticky dough.

3 Divide the dough in half and place on a lightly floured surface. Lightly knead each piece just to bring each one together into a smooth ball, then pat each ball down and roll into a circle about 1cm thick. Cut each circle into quarters (rather like farls).

4 Heat a griddle or heavy-based frying pan over a medium heat, then lightly grease with butter. Cook the scones in batches for about 5 minutes on each side until evenly browned, then transfer to a wire cooling rack to cool. Eat as fresh as possible.

Loved by Alfie

'They're right and tasty.'

Your New Favourite French Toast

This recipe will be your new go-to with its lovely crisp exterior and soft centre. The magic ingredient is flour and I'm pretty sure you will already have all the ingredients in your cupboard and fridge. The best part of this breakfast is getting to go wild with the toppings. I haven't looked back since I discovered how wonderful bacon and maple syrup are together. Some fresh strawberries, maple syrup, icing sugar and fresh cream is also hard to beat.

SERVES 4

1 large egg
30g salted butter, melted, plus extra for cooking
185ml whole milk
2 tsp vanilla extract
40g plain flour
25g caster sugar
pinch of salt
pinch of ground cinnamon (optional)
pinch of ground nutmeg (optional)
1 brioche loaf

1. Beat the egg in a wide dish, then add the melted butter and whisk through. Gradually add the milk, whisking to combine, then add the vanilla.
2. Add the flour, sugar, salt and spices (if using) to a separate bowl and whisk to combine. Gradually add to your egg mixture, continuing to whisk until smooth.
3. Slice your brioche loaf into generous slices.
4. Heat a frying pan or griddle over a medium heat and melt a knob of butter in the pan. Soak both sides of your brioche slices for about 15–20 seconds in the milk mixture (you will need to cook in batches). Place each slice in the pan and cook for about a minute on each side, or until golden.
5. Serve immediately or place on a wire cooling rack with a few sheets of kitchen paper. Enjoy with your favourite toppings. If you have any leftovers, which is highly unlikely, you can reheat them in the toaster just like a slice of toast, or for 5–10 minutes in an oven heated to 130°C fan/150°C/gas 2.

Apple Potato Bread

You might never have heard of apple potato bread and question whether it works, but trust me it does. It's getting harder and harder to find and only a few local bakeries near me still have it. It's a real traditional Northern Irish bake of a hearty potato bread casing stuffed with lovely sweet, tart apples, and my dad could eat it until the cows come home.

SERVES 2

- 600g cold mashed potato
- ¼ tsp baking powder
- ¼ tsp salt
- 40g salted butter, melted
- 100g plain flour, plus extra for dusting
- 2 Bramley apples, peeled, cored and thinly sliced
- 50g caster sugar

1. Add the mashed potato to a mixing bowl along with the baking powder and salt. Pour in the melted butter and combine with a spoon, then sift in the flour and mix until combined and smooth.
2. Pop the dough onto a lightly floured surface and gently knead until it comes together to form a smooth ball. Divide this in half and roll each into a circle about 5mm thick.
3. Gently heat the apple slices in a saucepan with the sugar for a few minutes to soften, but make sure not to stew them (this step is optional).
4. Add the apples to one side of each circle of dough, dividing them equally, then sprinkle each pile with half of the sugar (if you didn't already use it to soften the apples). Fold the dough over to cover the filling and seal the edges by pressing with your thumb. Lightly flour the top of each parcel.
5. Heat a griddle or dry frying pan over a medium heat. Place each potato bread parcel, floured-side down, onto your pan and lightly flour the new top sides as well. Cook for around 15 minutes on each side until a nice crust forms.
6. You can allow them to cool on a wire cooling rack and eat later, or serve immediately. They pair brilliantly with some fresh cream and lemon curd. This is such a niche Northern Irish bake and I think you will love it once you give it a try.

Loved by Alfie

'Reminds me of the old days.'

Breads

Wheaten Bread Loaf

This bread is known by so many names. In Northern Ireland I've always known it as wheaten bread. When I played with Connacht in Galway City, it was called soda bread or brown bread. I learnt this one day when I ordered a sandwich on brown bread and they looked at me funny. I was expecting some brown pan loaf, but got served an open sandwich on wheaten bread. My mate Tommy explained that that's what brown bread was in the south of Ireland. When I was young, I'd have done the same with slaps of ham and buckets of coleslaw on some homemade wheaten bread. Like they say, every day is a school day.

MAKES 2 SMALL LOAVES

340g coarse wholemeal flour
170g plain flour
2 tsp sugar (any type)
55g salted butter, softened
2 tsp bicarbonate of soda
600ml buttermilk
handful of rolled oats

1 Preheat the oven to 150°C fan/170°C/gas 4 and line two 450g (1lb) loaf tins with baking paper.

2 Add the coarse wholemeal flour and plain flour to a mixing bowl along with the sugar. Rub the butter throughout the mix using your fingertips. Do this until it's fully combined and it slightly resembles dry breadcrumbs. Add the bicarbonate of soda and mix this in.

3 Gradually add the buttermilk, mixing with a fork between each addition until you have a sticky but workable consistency.

4 Divide the mixture between your lined loaf tins and spread evenly. You can be particular and weigh the mixtures, but as long as they're similar enough you're sweet. Put a crease up the middle of each mixture using the back of a teaspoon – this helps to stop it rising too much and cracking in the middle. Sprinkle the tops with oats.

5 Bake for 40–45 minutes until lightly golden on top and cooked through. You can check this by inserting a skewer into the centres – if it comes out clean, it's good to go.

6 Allow them to cool in the tins for about 30 minutes and then fully on a wire cooling rack. Now you can slice 'em up and get stuck in. My favourite way to have this is toasted with real butter and homemade jam, but it goes with everything if you ask me.

Irish Batch Loaf

This loaf is native to Ireland and gets its name from coming in batches of two, four or even more. You can pull them apart and get stuck in. This bread is soft and pillowy with an iconic, chewy, blackened top. People may think it's burnt, but that black top is the best part – adding so much flavour. When we were younger, mum would allow me and my wee sister Emma to toast a few slices of this against the fire. That toast, dripping with real butter and homemade jam, was something else and a memory I cherish.

MAKES 4 SMALL BATCH LOAVES

450ml lukewarm water
10g (1 tbsp) instant dried (fast-action) yeast
35g beef dripping or lard, melted
650g strong white flour, sifted, plus extra for dusting
10g (1¾ tsp) fine salt
vegetable oil, for greasing

1 Divide the lukewarm water equally between two separate bowls. Add the dried yeast to one and the melted beef dripping or lard to the other. Give them a mix and allow to sit for 5 minutes.

2 Add the flour and salt to a large mixing bowl and whisk to combine. Now add both the yeast and dripping mixtures and mix with a fork until fully incorporated and no dry bits are left. After a while, you'll probably find it easier to get your hands stuck in.

3 At this point, you can either knead it in a stand mixer fitted with a dough hook for about 10–15 minutes until it's pillowy soft to touch and the gluten has built up, so it's stretchy. Alternatively, get it onto a lightly floured work surface and knead well by hand (see page 12). Shape it into a smooth ball, pop it into a lightly oiled bowl and cover with some cling film. Leave to rise for 1–2 hours, or until doubled in size. This will depend on the temperature of where you place it. On a windowsill on a moderately warm day is perfect.

4 Once it has doubled in size, knock the air out of your dough by giving it a gentle press with your fist. Divide into 4 equal pieces. Shape these into balls by flattening and then pulling the edges into the middle. Tighten these edges that now meet in the middle of your dough by pinching with your fingers. Flip it over and roll vigorously in a circle motion with a claw-shaped hand.

5 Arrange each ball next to one other in a lightly greased square loaf tin. Alternatively, place two balls in the same fashion into a lightly greased 900g (2lb) loaf tin. Cover with some cling film and leave to prove again until doubled in size.

6 Preheat the oven to 240°C fan/260°C/gas 10. Add a baking tin to the shelf below where you will place the loaves. Just before you add your loaves to the oven, pour about 2 cups of boiling water into the baking tray, and then immediately add your loaves to the oven. This added steam is what creates the beautiful dark crust.

7 Bake the loaves for 20 minutes, then remove the tray of water. If you are using two loaf tins to bake your loaves, it will take between 10–15 minutes more to finish baking. If you are baking in one single square loaf tin, it will take another 20–25 minutes. They want to be very dark brown, almost black, on top and sound hollow when tapped on the bottom.

8 Once baked, remove the loaves from the tin and allow to cool on a wire cooling rack before slicing. This is best eaten warm with butter and jam, but it's equally as delicious packed with some thick-cut ham, cheese and pickle.

Potato Farls

Also known as potato bread, spud bread, tattie bread, taddie bread, fadge, slims ... the list goes on, these were traditionally made with leftover mashed potato, so nothing would go to waste. The term farls comes from an early Scots word, fardell, meaning a fourth or quarter, which is why the Ulster Scots lay claim to my favourite bread. I was a bit of a fiend for the stuff when I was young. Whenever we had a fry up, I'd swap some of my bacon or sausages to get more potato bread, then plaster it in red sauce. Start making these for yourself and you'll have the same problem.

MAKES 4

- 450g leftover cooked mashed potato (still warm, if possible)
- 60g butter
- 1 tsp salt
- 120g self-raising flour, sifted, plus extra for dusting

1. Place the leftover mashed potato in a bowl. Ideally, you want the mash to be slightly warm, so the butter combines well. Add the butter and salt, then give this a good mash until it's fully combined and smooth.
2. Gradually add the flour to the mash, mixing well between each addition until it is all combined.
3. Turn the mixture out onto a lightly floured surface and gently bring it together into a ball. Pat it down into a flat circle, about 1cm thick. Lightly dust the top with flour, then cut it into quarters.
4. Heat a griddle or dry frying pan over a medium heat, then get your farls onto the pan, floured sides down. Dust the tops with a bit more flour, then cook for about 5–6 minutes on each side until they form a nice crust.
5. Remove from the pan and allow to cool on a wire cooling rack. These are very soft and delicate when fresh, so you can allow them to firm up a little.
6. You can have these immediately with some butter plastered over them, but be prepared for it to run down your chin. You can also toast them later. The best way to serve them is fried in the pan along with a big fry up. The only question is, which sauce: red or brown? Or, if we're getting really fancy, what about some of that Ballymaloe Relish?

Soda Farls

Soda farls are another classic from my neck of the woods and they're surprisingly versatile. Generally, they would be eaten plain with some butter and jam, or a few slices of ham and cheese. Or, most commonly, in an Ulster Fry, along with Potato Farls (page 43). Another tasty one is a filled soda, fried up and filled with bacon, sausage and egg.

MAKES 4

370g self-raising soda bread flour, plus extra for dusting
285ml buttermilk
1 tbsp vegetable oil

1. Sift the flour into a mixing bowl.
2. Pour the buttermilk into a jug along with the vegetable oil and give this a mix.
3. Gradually add the buttermilk mixture to the flour, mixing between each addition with a fork. You don't want the mixture to be too wet, it should just come together and there should be no to very little dry flour left.
4. Bring the dough together on a floured work surface, shaping it into a circle shape about 2cm thick. You can start this with your hands, patting it down, and then use a rolling pin. Cut this into quarters to form your farls.
5. Dust the tops of the farls with some flour. Place floured side down on a griddle or dry frying pan set over a medium heat. Dust the tops with a little more flour for when you flip them. Bake each side for 10–15 minutes until it forms a nice crust. Finally, you can do the edges for a few minutes just to seal them nicely and avoid any raw pieces. Do this by propping them up on each other, or rolling and holding them with your hands.
6. Transfer to a wire cooling rack and loosely cover with a light tea towel. Let them cool before slicing them up. Then it's up to you – butter and jam? Or are you getting the pan on and making an Ulster Fry for everyone?

Loved by Alfie

'I had them fresh off the griddle at my Granny's. The butter would have been dripping down our chins.'

Wheaten Farls

Unlike wheaten bread (page 38), which is known throughout the Emerald Isle, wheaten farls are native to Northern Ireland. These are delicious with some real butter and jam or even a few big chunky slices of cheese. My Dad will also argue with his shadow that these are a staple in an Ulster fry. We could sit all night over a few creamy pints of Guinness, twistin' over what goes into our native fry ups – Ulster, Irish, Scottish and English. But then, when you have this fried up, you'll probably agree with Big Mel.

MAKES 4

370g wheaten bread mix (store-bought or use a 2:1 mix of coarse wholemeal flour to plain flour), plus extra for dusting
285ml buttermilk
1 tbsp vegetable oil

1 Add the wheaten bread mix to a bowl.

2 Pour the buttermilk into a jug along with the vegetable oil and give it a bit of a mix. Gradually pour this into the bowl, stirring with a fork between each addition. Continue to do this until you get a nice, soft and slightly sticky dough.

3 Turn it onto a lightly floured work surface and lightly bring together with your hands. Shape into a circle about 2.5cm thick. Do this by patting it down with your hands or use a floured rolling pin. Cut into quarters to make your farls, dusting the tops with some more of your flour mix.

4 Place the farls, floured side down, on a griddle or dry frying pan set over a medium heat. Bake for about 10–15 minutes on each side, or until they form a nice crust. Dust the tops with a little more flour when you flip them. Once you have both sides done, roll them onto their edges just to seal them a little.

5 Transfer to a wire cooling rack, loosely cover with a light tea towel and leave to cool a little.

6 Get them sliced up and enjoy with some real butter and jam, or however you like.

Traditional Farmhouse Loaf

I've always loved a good farmhouse loaf – soft and fluffy on the inside with a lovely chewy crust. You might think making your own bread isn't worth the bother, but the difference in flavour and texture is huge. Look at a store-bought equivalent and you can't even pronounce some of the ingredients on the label – well, I can't. Yes, it might not last as long and it could do with toasting on the third day, but that's the way bread should be. Once you try this loaf on a lazy weekend, you won't be heading to the shops for bread anytime soon.

MAKES 1 LOAF

600g strong white bread flour, plus extra for dusting
2 tsp salt
1 tsp caster sugar
5g (1½ tsp) instant dried (fast-action) yeast
50g unsalted butter, softened
350ml lukewarm water
vegetable oil, for greasing

1 Add all the ingredients (except the oil) to a stand mixer fitted with a dough hook and mix on a medium–low speed for about 10 minutes until the dough is smooth and elastic. If you're kneading by hand, add the flour, salt, sugar, yeast and butter to a large mixing bowl, make a well in the middle with a spoon, then add a little water and mix thoroughly. Continue to add the water, gradually mixing until it has formed a ball of dough. Transfer to a lightly floured surface and knead for about 10 minutes until it's smooth and elastic.

2 Place the dough into a large, lightly oiled bowl and cover with a clean tea towel or cling film. Leave to rise for about 1½ hours, or until it has doubled in size.

3 Grease a 900g (2lb) loaf tin with a little oil, then lightly oil a clean work surface. Pop your proved dough onto the work surface and shape into a rectangle, roughly the same width as the tin. Roll the dough up from the widest side, making sure it's nice and tight. If the roll is too loose, you will end up with big air pockets in your loaf. Pinch the seams together and place in the tin, seam-side down. Cover and leave to prove in a warm spot for a further 45 minutes.

4 Meanwhile, preheat the oven to 210°C fan/230°C/gas 8 and place a shallow baking tin at the bottom. Boil the kettle.

5 With a sharp, oiled knife, make 3 slashes, about 1cm deep, across the top of the loaf and lightly dust the top with some flour. Place on the middle shelf of the oven and quickly pour a cup of boiling water into the hot baking tin. Close the oven door as soon as possible to keep the steam in – this will help develop that lovely crust. Bake for 10 minutes before reducing the temperature to 180°C fan/200°C/gas 6 and baking for a further 30–35 minutes (see tip).

6 Transfer to a wire cooling rack and allow to cool before slicing.

Top Tip

Once baked, the loaf should sound hollow when you tap the bottom. You can also check the internal temperature if you have a food thermometer – it should read around 90–95°C when done.

No-Knead Bread

This bread takes all the hassle out of kneading and is the closest thing I've had to a sourdough without all that starter carry on. You don't have to worry about keeping a starter alive and it takes minimal work. All you have to do is let it sit overnight. It has a lovely chewy crust along with those big air pockets you see in sourdough.

MAKES 1 LOAF

430g strong white flour or bread flour, plus extra for dusting
1g (generous ¼ tsp) instant dried (fast-action) yeast
8g (2 tsp) salt
345ml water

1. Add the flour, dried yeast and salt to a large mixing bowl. Give this a gentle whisk together to combine, then pour in the water, stirring until it forms a shaggy dough. Cover with some cling film and leave to rest at room temperature for about 12–18 hours. The surface will become spotted and bubbly when ready.
2. Turn the dough out onto a lightly floured work surface and dust it with some more flour. Fold it over on itself a few times, then cover again with some cling film and leave it on the work surface for 15 minutes.
3. Using just enough flour so the dough doesn't stick to your hands, gently and quickly shape your dough into a ball. Leave it seam-side down, dust with some more flour, cover with a clean tea towel and allow to prove for a further 2 hours.
4. About 30 minutes before it's finished proving, preheat the oven to 210°C fan/230°C/gas 8 and put a Dutch oven or heavy pot with a lid into the oven to heat up.
5. Carefully remove your pot from the oven and place the dough, seam-side up, into the pot. Dust it again with flour and don't worry if it looks a bit messy – it will sort itself out.
6. Bake with the lid on for 30 minutes, then remove the lid and bake for a further 15–20 minutes, or until it's golden brown and has formed a nice crust.
7. Transfer to a wire cooling rack and leave to cool fully. Now slice it up and plaster it in some real butter and homemade jam, if you fancy it.

Belfast Baps

Originally, the Belfast bap was created to feed the poor of Belfast during the times of the famine. Now it has become an institution in parts of the city and all the local bakeries bake them. Known for their large size and thick, chewy, almost burnt tops, you'd think they were a loaf from the sheer heft of them. Nowadays, they are served filled to the throat with breakfast items, such as bacon, sausage, black pudding and a fried egg. My Dad always said when he had one for the 10 o'clock tae in work, you wouldn't need another bite a' meat until that night. He loves them.

MAKES 4

480ml lukewarm water
2 tsp salt
2 tsp sugar (any type)
2 tbsp instant dried (fast-action) yeast
780g strong white flour, plus extra for dusting
vegetable oil, for greasing
rice flour, for dusting

1 Add the lukewarm water to a large mixing bowl along with the salt, sugar and yeast. Stir to dissolve and allow to sit for about 5 minutes.

2 Add half of the flour and mix until smooth, then gradually add the rest of the flour until the dough starts to pull away from the sides of the bowl.

3 Either knead the dough in a stand mixer fitted with a dough hook for about 7–10 minutes until it is smooth and elastic, or place it on a lightly floured work surface and knead by hand (see page 12).

4 Shape the dough into a ball, place in a lightly oiled bowl and cover with cling film. Leave to rise for about 1 hour until doubled in size.

5 Gently punch the air out of your dough using a clenched fist and divide into 4 equal pieces. Shape these into balls by pulling the edges into the middle and pinching them tight, then roll in a circular motion with a claw-shaped hand. Line a baking tray with greaseproof paper and place the dough balls on the tray, leaving a few centimetres between each one. Cover with some lightly oiled cling film and leave to prove for another 30 minutes until puffy.

6 Meanwhile, preheat the oven to 180°C fan/200°C/gas 6.

7 Remove the cling film and sprinkle the tops with some rice flour.

8 Bake for 30 minutes. Turn the grill on for the last 5 minutes of baking, but keep an eye on them. You want the top to be a deep brown (this is a matter of preference – some like the top lighter and others like it a shade before burnt) but you don't want them to actually burn. When you tap the bases they should sound hollow.

9 Leave to cool on a wire cooling rack while you work out what you're going to fill them with.

Blaa Baps

These originate from Waterford and are a delicious white bread roll. You can't go wrong with a fresh blaa bap, plastered in butter and filled to the gills with whatever you're in the mood for, whether that's some sausages lathered in red sauce or some boiled ham, thick cuts of cheese and some pickle. I'm making myself hungry here, so I'd probably have two!

MAKES 12

- 440ml lukewarm water, or as needed
- 1 tsp caster sugar
- 14g (4½ tsp) instant dried (fast-action) yeast
- 780g strong white bread flour, plus extra for dusting
- 1 tsp salt
- vegetable oil, for greasing

1. In a bowl or jug, combine 140ml of the lukewarm water with the sugar and yeast, stirring until dissolved. Leave to sit for around 5 minutes to activate the yeast – it will start to froth and bubble.
2. In a large mixing bowl, combine the flour and salt, mixing well. Add the activated yeast and stir with a large spoon. Gradually add the remaining water, stirring until all the dry ingredients are incorporated and a ball of dough has formed, leaving the bottom of the bowl clean. You may need less or more water, depending on your flour. You can also do this in a stand mixer fitted with a dough hook.
3. Once you have a nice clean dough ball, knead (either in the stand mixer on medium speed or on a lightly floured work surface) for around 5 minutes until smooth and elastic. Pop the dough into a large, lightly oiled bowl. Cover with a tea towel or cling film and leave to rise in a warm place for 1 hour, or until doubled in size.
4. Gently knock the air out of your dough with a clenched fist. Gently shape back into a ball, place back in your bowl, then cover and prove again until doubled in size, about 30 minutes.
5. Loosely line a 23 x 33cm (9 x 13in) baking tin with a large piece of greaseproof paper, leaving an overhang. Turn the dough out onto a lightly floured surface and gently divide into 12 equal pieces using a knife. Each piece should weigh around 90g. Roll each piece of dough between your palms to create a nice round shape. Place each roll in the prepared tin, spaced about 2.5cm apart. Cover with a clean tea towel or cling film and prove for 45 minutes–1 hour.
6. Meanwhile preheat the oven to 190°C fan/210°C/gas 6.
7. Lightly dust the tops of the rolls with some flour and bake for about 25–30 minutes. The rolls will develop crisp bottoms when fully baked and should be light on top, not too brown.
8. Remove from the tin and allow to cool on a wire cooling rack.

Veda Malted Bread

Veda bread is one of those things I was reared on. If you aren't from Northern Ireland or haven't had the pleasure of visiting, you're probably wondering what it is! I can only describe it as the best malt loaf there is. It's almost chewy in texture and if you really want to take it to the next level get a big wedge of cheese on there. Just like potato and soda farls, this stuff is like currency to any Northern Irish person living abroad. I hope this recipe brings a wee slice of home to you.

MAKES 1 LOAF

25g unsalted butter, plus extra (melted) for greasing and brushing
15g soft dark brown sugar
60g malt extract
30g black treacle
230ml water
350g strong white bread flour
100g malt flour (if you can't get malt flour, just replace with more strong white bread flour)
12g (4 tsp) instant dried (fast-action) yeast
5g (generous ¾ tsp) salt
whole milk, for brushing

1 In a medium saucepan, melt together the butter, sugar, malt extract and black treacle over a low heat. Stir every so often, to ensure it doesn't stick or burn. Once melted, add the water and mix until combined. Set aside to cool for about 5 minutes.

2 In the bowl of a stand mixer fitted with a dough hook, combine the flours, yeast and salt. Now pour in the wet ingredients and knead for 8–10 minutes until smooth. (You can also mix these ingredients in a large bowl, then knead on a lightly floured surface. It will just take a bit of elbow grease.)

3 Lightly grease a 900g (2lb) loaf tin. Shape the dough into an oblong and place in the tin. Loosely cover with a clean tea towel or some cling film, and leave to rise for 1–1½ hours, or until doubled in size. If you press it with a fingertip, it should spring back slowly, leaving a mark about half the size.

4 Meanwhile, preheat the oven to 180°C fan/200°C/gas 6.

5 Once doubled in size, gently brush the top of the loaf with some milk and bake for about 35–40 minutes. It is ready when the top has a deep caramel colour and it sounds hollow when tapped on the bottom.

6 Remove from the tin and place on a wire cooling rack, then immediately brush with some melted butter. Allow to cool fully before slicing. I've always loved this toasted, lathered with real butter, with a few thick slices of Cheddar cheese.

Fruit Bannock

This is a proper traditional bread at home in Northern Ireland. You might also know it as fruit soda, but either way it's delicious. Filled with juicy sultanas, this is hard to beat – fresh or toasted. I think I could live off this stuff and when you try it you'll understand why.

MAKES 1 LOAF

- 455g soda bread flour (or plain flour with 1 tsp bicarbonate of soda), plus extra for dusting
- 60g salted butter
- 115g caster sugar
- 170g sultanas (check any stalks have been removed)
- 2 eggs, lightly beaten
- 275ml buttermilk

1. Preheat the oven to 180°C fan/200°C/gas 6.
2. Add the soda bread flour to a large mixing bowl. Add the butter and work it into the flour using your fingertips. Don't squeeze it, just press it through your fingertips, allowing the air into it.
3. Add the sugar and work this through in the same fashion.
4. Add your sultanas and mix them evenly throughout.
5. Add the eggs and combine well.
6. Gradually add your buttermilk, mixing between each addition. It will give you a slightly sticky but workable dough.
7. Pop the dough onto a lightly floured work surface and shape it into a ball. Pat it down into a circle about 4cm thick and dust the top with a little bit of flour.
8. You can bake it on a lightly floured baking tray or use a perforated pie dish, if you have one. Mark a cross in the middle of your bannock using a floured wooden spoon, about 1cm deep.
9. Bake for about 40 minutes, or until it's lightly golden on top and sounds hollow when tapped on the bottom.
10. Transfer to a wire cooling rack and let it cool fully before slicing. Get it plastered in some real butter and some homemade jam!

Loved by Alfie

'Wet the cup. I'd be fond of a slice or two of this now.'

Biscuits and Small Bites

Shortbread

This is a staple in our house, made at least once a month because it's seriously delicious. Try this once and you'll be comparing your favourite store-bought shortbread to a breeze block. This is like eating butter – it melts in your mouth. My Granda Alfie can judge how good shortbread is by its colour. He has it down to a tee. He should be a judge on that TV baking show we all love. He's had more baked goods than I've had hot dinners!

MAKES ABOUT 36 PIECES

340g salted butter, softened
170g caster sugar, plus extra for sprinkling
225g plain flour, plus extra for dusting
170g cornflour

1 Cream together the softened butter and sugar in a bowl until pale and fluffy. You can do this in a stand mixer or with a hand mixer. (To really have the arms hanging off ye, use a wooden spoon. But unless you want it to take a month of Sundays, swallow your pride and get the machines out.)

2 Sift the plain flour and cornflour into this and beat the lot together. It will start to form a slight crumb. Now bring it all together into a ball with your hands, wrap in cling film and chill in the fridge for around 20–30 minutes.

3 Preheat the oven to 140°C fan/160°C/gas 3. Line a large baking tray with greaseproof paper.

4 Unwrap the chilled ball of dough, place on a lightly floured surface and cut it in half (this is just to make things easier when you roll it out and you can cook the biscuits in batches). Shape the dough into a circle with your hands, then roll it out to around 5mm thick. With a floured 6cm pastry cutter or glass, cut out your shortbread biscuits. You can even use wee shaped cutters depending on the time of year. We're talkin' Easter, Halloween, Christmas, etc.

5 Pop the shapes onto the prepared baking tray and prick the top of each one a few times with a fork. Bake for about 15–20 minutes until lightly coloured on top. You want it to be lightly golden, not a dark colour.

6 Remove from the oven, transfer to a wire cooling rack and sprinkle with some caster sugar. Once they've cooled, they're ready to be inhaled.

Loved by Alfie

'I know my shortbread and this stuff looks the part!'

Tosset Cake

You could compare these biscuits to shortbread, but they are a great change. They hail from over the water in England and are quickly becoming a forgotten classic. I know they aren't from my wheelhouse of local recipes, but my nanny loves them. She would regularly rustle up a batch to go with an afternoon coffee or tea, or for those unannounced guests who always pop in.

MAKES 25

500g plain flour, plus extra for dusting
150g caster sugar, plus extra for sprinkling
500g unsalted butter, cubed and softened
1 heaped tsp caraway seeds
1 heaped tsp coriander seeds
icing sugar, to decorate

1 Sift the flour and sugar into a large bowl, then add the butter and rub in using your fingertips. It will eventually resemble a breadcrumb texture.

2 Add the seeds to a pestle and mortar and lightly crush them. Add the crushed seeds to the bowl and stir to combine. Bring the mixture together to form a ball of dough using your hands, wrap in clingfilm and place in the fridge for 1 hour to chill.

3 Preheat the oven to 160°C fan/180°C/gas 4.

4 Place the chilled dough on a lightly floured surface and roll out to about 5mm thick. With a floured 6cm pastry cutter, cut your tosset cakes out and place them on a baking tray lightly dusted with flour. Sprinkle the tops with a little bit of sugar.

5 Bake for 10–15 minutes, or until firm and a nice pale colour. You don't want them to brown or become overly golden. Once baked, pop them onto a wire cooling rack and allow to cool completely.

6 Dust with some icing sugar to finish. These are a delicious wee treat with a brew and are perfect to have ready for any visitor.

Crunchies

These wee buns remind me of one of my favourite biscuits (gypsy creams), but – like everything – when they're homemade, they taste so much better. My nanny made these all the time when we were young and I only recently discovered that she helped make them in a local bakery many years ago. They have a lovely crunch, hence the name, and almost taste golden, if you get me.

MAKES 16–18

225g salted butter, softened
170g caster sugar
4 tsp golden syrup
1 tsp vanilla extract
225g plain flour, plus extra for dusting
2 tsp baking powder
1 tsp bicarbonate of soda
30g desiccated coconut
200g flakemeal (rolled oats)

For the buttercream
85g salted butter, softened
140g icing sugar, sifted
1 tsp vanilla extract
3 squares of white chocolate, melted

To decorate
100–200g milk chocolate, melted

Loved by Alfie

'Mamie thinks these are made too big, but I think the bigger the better!'

1 Preheat the oven to 140°C fan/160°C/gas 3 and line a baking tray or two with baking paper.

2 Pop the butter and sugar into a mixing bowl and cream together until soft and fluffy. Add the golden syrup and vanilla extract, beating them through.

3 Add all your dry ingredients to a separate bowl, mixing them all together. Pop this into your butter mixture and gently mix it together until combined.

4 Dust your hands with a little flour, then take about 25g of your mixture and roll it into a ball, about the size of a walnut. Repeat until all the mixture is used up. Pop them onto the prepared baking tray, spaced about 3cm apart.

5 Bake for about 15 minutes, or until slightly golden on top.

6 Allow to cool on the trays for about 5 minutes before transferring to a wire cooling rack.

7 Meanwhile, make your buttercream. Beat the butter and icing sugar together until smooth and fluffy. Add the vanilla extract and melted white chocolate, then beat again until combined.

8 Once cooled, match each crunchie up to its best pair. Sandwich these together with your buttercream and place on a tray. Drizzle some melted milk chocolate over each crunchie, using a disposable piping bag or even just a spoon. Let the chocolate firm up, then dig in and enjoy!

Triple Chocolate Cookies

There are few things better than a fresh cookie with a cold glass of milk and these triple chocolate cookies tick all the boxes. Crisp exterior with that slight chewy centre, the way all cookies should be if you're asking me. This recipe hits all three of your chocolates, so it keeps everyone happy and if there's a certain type you prefer you can easily adjust accordingly.

MAKES ABOUT 20

150g milk chocolate
200g salted butter, softened
110g caster sugar
90g soft light brown or muscovado sugar
1 large egg plus 1 egg yolk, lightly beaten
1 tbsp vanilla extract
260g plain flour
40g cocoa powder
1½ tsp bicarbonate of soda
pinch of salt
50g dark chocolate, chopped
100g white chocolate, chopped

1. Melt 100g of the milk chocolate over a bain-marie or in short 30-second bursts in the microwave, stirring in between. When melted, set aside and allow to cool. Chop the remaining 50g milk chocolate and set aside.
2. Cream together the butter and sugars until pale and fluffy. This should take about 3–4 minutes in a stand mixer. Add the egg and egg yolk along with the vanilla extract, beating until fully combined.
3. Add the flour, cocoa powder, bicarbonate of soda and salt to a bowl and gently whisk to combine. Sift this into the creamed mixture and gently beat until fully incorporated and smooth. Add the melted chocolate and fold through with a spatula until combined.
4. Add the chopped milk, dark and white chocolates, mixing until these are evenly distributed throughout.
5. There are two ways to do this next stage: Either chill your dough in the fridge for at least 1 hour, then scoop a few tablespoons onto your lined baking sheets and bake. Alternatively, wrap your dough in cling film and roll into a 5cm-thick sausage shape. It may be easier to do this in 2 batches. Chill for at least 1 hour in the fridge.
6. Meanwhile, preheat the oven to 170°C fan/190°C/gas 5. Line a baking sheet with greaseproof paper.
7. Remove the dough from the fridge and use a sharp knife to slice into rounds about 1.5cm thick. Pop the rounds onto the prepared baking sheet, leaving space for them to double in size. Bake for 8–10 minutes until slightly crisp at the edges but still soft in the middle.
8. Remove from the oven and leave to cool on the tray for about 10 minutes. Transfer to a wire cooling rack to cool fully. These are a treat when slightly warm with a glass of fresh, cold milk.

Flakemeal Biscuits

A lot of people will downplay how good these wee oat bickies are. Yes, they're old school and remind you of your granny's house, but let's be honest – that's what it's all about. When I'm having a wee treat, I want to be transported back to a point in my life, and what's better than being a youngin', horsin' these into ye with a cuppa tae in your granny's kitchen?

MAKES ABOUT 36

225g salted butter
115g caster sugar
170g plain flour, plus extra for dusting
30g desiccated coconut
200g porridge oats (flakemeal)
pinch of bicarbonate of soda
pinch of salt

To decorate
sprinkle of caster sugar
100g chocolate of choice, melted
100g walnuts, chopped or left in halves

1. Beat together the butter and sugar in a large bowl, scraping down the edges until it's fully creamed and smooth.
2. In a separate bowl, combine the flour, coconut, oats, bicarb and salt. Gradually add these to your creamed butter and sugar, mixing well between each addition and scraping down with a spatula until thoroughly combined.
3. Scoop the dough out onto some cling film, wrap it up and chill in the fridge for about 45 minutes.
4. Preheat the oven to 150°C fan/170°C/gas 3. Line several baking trays with baking paper.
5. On a lightly floured surface, cut the chilled dough in half and roll each piece out to about 5mm thick. Cut your biscuits out with a floured 6cm pastry cutter and place them on the lined trays. Prick the tops of your biscuits a few times with a fork.
6. Bake for about 25–30 minutes, or until slightly browned on top and cooked through. Let them sit on the trays for about 5 minutes before removing to a wire cooling rack to cool fully.
7. Now you can top them whatever way you'd prefer. The traditional way is to sprinkle them with caster sugar, but a wee drop of melted chocolate and some chopped walnuts or walnut halves is another great topping. You can put your own twist on them at this point, so don't hold back.

Loved by Alfie

'Simple but effective.'

Empire Biscuits

These are a nice butter biscuit, sandwiched together with some raspberry jam, topped with a little icing and your chosen decoration. Sounds simple, I know, but it's the simple things that really hit the spot, if you ask me. And if you're asking my nanny, she loves them a few days after baking, when they aren't as crunchy – just at that perfect stage of slightly crisp but not soft. My mum and wee sister Emma nearly fight over these when they're dropped off at the house, that's how sought after they are.

MAKES 24

250g plain flour, plus extra for dusting
50g cornflour
100g caster sugar
175g salted butter, cubed

To decorate
100g Raspberry Jam (store-bought or see page 215)
250g icing sugar
2 tbsp warm water
toppings of choice (desiccated coconut, sprinkles, jelly sweets, sugar-coated chocolate drops, etc.)

Loved by Alfie

'These never last long in this house!'

1 Preheat the oven to 140°C fan/160°C/gas 3 and line a baking tray or two with baking paper.

2 Place the flour and cornflour into a food processor and blitz to combine. You can also do this in a bowl using your hands, but it's handier to let the machine do the work. Add the sugar and give it another wee blitz, or mix in your bowl. Gradually add the butter while mixing in the food processor – it will start to come together at this point. Transfer it to a bowl and use your hands to get it fully combined into a ball. If you're going without the food processor, gradually add the butter and rub it into the dry ingredients using your fingertips. It will resemble breadcrumbs as you work through it. Keep doing this until it's all combined, then form it into a ball.

3 Transfer the dough to a lightly floured work surface and make sure it's fully combined by lightly kneading the dough. Roll out with a flour-dusted rolling pin (or even a clean wine bottle) to about 5mm thick. Use a floured 5cm pastry cutter or glass to cut out 48 biscuit shapes. Place them on the prepared baking tray/s, pricking each biscuit a few times with a fork.

4 Bake for about 20–25 minutes, or until the biscuits are slightly golden on top. Allow them to cool fully on a wire cooling rack before trying your best to match each biscuit up to a similar pair.

5 Spread a 5mm layer of jam between each of your biscuit pairs and sandwich them together.

6 Mix the icing sugar in a large bowl with the warm water until it's smooth. Spread a dollop of icing on top of each biscuit, then freestyle on the decorations.

Coffee Kisses

Nanny and Granda love a coffee, and when they discovered these biscuits they were hooked. They're so simple to make and take no time at all. If you're a fan of that distinct coffee flavour, you will love these delightful wee biscuits.

MAKES ABOUT 20

125g caster sugar
1 egg, lightly beaten
1 tbsp instant coffee
1–2 tbsp iced water
375g self-raising flour, plus extra for dusting
160g unsalted butter, chopped
100g white chocolate, melted

For the coffee buttercream
80g unsalted butter, softened
125g icing sugar
2 tsp water
2 tsp instant coffee

1. Preheat the oven to 160°C fan/180°C/gas 4 and line 2 baking trays with baking paper.
2. Add the sugar, egg, coffee and water to a bowl and mix together until combined. Set this aside.
3. Sift the flour into a large bowl, add the butter and rub this into the flour using your fingertips. It will resemble fine breadcrumbs.
4. Now add your wet ingredients and mix with a fork to form a soft dough.
5. Pop the dough onto a lightly floured surface and lightly knead until smooth. Roll out the dough between 2 sheets of greaseproof paper to about 5mm thick. Using a floured 5–6cm fluted pastry/cookie cutter, cut out biscuits and place on the prepared baking trays. Lightly knead any excess and re-roll and cut until you've used all your dough.
6. Bake for about 10 minutes, or until lightly golden on top. Once baked, place them on a wire cooling rack and allow to cool.
7. For the coffee buttercream, beat the butter and icing sugar together until pale and creamy. Combine the water and coffee in a small bowl and add this to the creamed butter mixture. Beat this until it's fully combined and smooth. Add this to a piping bag with a nozzle.
8. Pipe buttercream over the inner side of one biscuit and then sandwich with another. Once you've piped all of your biscuits, drizzle with melted white chocolate and allow this to set. Now you can tuck in and enjoy these wee kisses of coffee flavour.

Chocolate-Coated Bourbon Creams

I feel the bourbon cream is underrated and doesn't get the love it deserves. But this recipe was inspired by my nanny, as she tried something similar from a shop recently and she couldn't get over how nice they were. We had to recreate them. I think we succeeded. I love a bourbon cream and the addition of a coating of chocolate just makes these classics that bit better.

MAKES 16

170g plain flour, sifted, plus extra for dusting
30g cocoa powder
85g salted butter, cubed
55g caster sugar, plus extra for sprinkling
2 tbsp golden syrup
1 egg, lightly beaten
400g milk chocolate, melted

For the buttercream
30g cocoa powder
2 tbsp boiling water
115g salted butter, softened
170g icing sugar, sifted

1 Sift the flour and cocoa powder into a large mixing bowl. Add the butter and rub in with your fingertips until it resembles fine breadcrumbs. Stir through the sugar and syrup, then gradually add the beaten egg, mixing with a fork until you have a firm dough.

2 Bring the dough together with your hands and turn out onto a lightly floured work surface. Gently roll into a rectangle shape, about 30 x 40cm. Cut in half lengthways, then cut each half into 16 fingers. Prick each piece of dough a few times with a fork. Carefully place on lined baking trays and refrigerate for 1 hour.

3 Meanwhile, preheat the oven to 160°C fan/180°C/gas 4.

4 Bake the biscuits for 10–15 minutes. Sprinkle with sugar when you remove them from the oven and let rest on the trays for a few minutes. Transfer them to a wire cooling rack to cool fully.

5 Meanwhile, make the buttercream. Dissolve the cocoa powder in the boiling water, mixing until smooth, and leave to cool. Cream the butter with the icing sugar until pale and smooth. Add the cooled cocoa mixture and beat until fully combined.

6 Match your biscuits to form pairs. Spread a layer of buttercream on one half, then sandwich together. Once you have them all filled and sandwiched, pop them into the fridge for about 45 minutes–1 hour.

7 Melt the chocolate over a bain-marie or in 30-second bursts in the microwave, stirring in between. Drop each biscuit into the melted chocolate, flipping with the help of 2 forks, until the whole biscuit is coated. Allow any excess chocolate to drip off into the bowl and place on a wire cooling rack with a tray beneath to catch any drips. Alternatively, place on a baking sheet lined with some greaseproof paper. Allow to set fully in the fridge and then get stuck in.

Marshmallow Fudge Tartlets

These easy-to-make little tartlets are 'bite size', if you have a mouth on ye like mine, and are one of my favourite wee buns to make. I'd happily polish off about five of these before the chocolate has had time to set.

MAKES 24

1 x batch of Shortcrust Pastry (store-bought or see page 212)
plain flour, for dusting
about 100g Raspberry Jam (store-bought or see page 215)
200g marshmallows
50–75g milk chocolate, roughly chopped

For the caramel fudge
115g salted butter
115g caster sugar
1 tbsp golden syrup
200g condensed milk

1 Preheat the oven to 150°C fan/170°C/gas 3.

2 Roll the pastry out on a lightly floured work surface to about 5mm thick. With a floured 6cm pastry cutter or glass, cut out 24 circles. Pop these into a couple of cupcake, tartlet or muffin tins and prick the base of each circle a few times with a fork. Bake for about 15–20 minutes until golden brown. Leave to rest in the tin for about 5 minutes, then transfer to a wire cooling rack to cool fully.

3 When cool, place ½ teaspoon of jam into each pastry shell.

4 Slice about a quarter off the tops of each marshmallow to make them fit the pastry shells (see tip) and pop them into each one.

5 To make the fudge caramel, put all of the ingredients into a heavy-based saucepan and melt over a medium heat. Bring to the boil, then gently simmer, stirring continuously to stop it catching on the base of the pan, for 5–10 minutes. The mixture will start to darken in colour and thicken up. When you get a nice fudgy consistency, remove from the heat. Be careful, as it will be very hot at this point.

6 Let the fudge caramel cool for a few moments to avoid melting the marshmallows, but ensure it's still a pourable consistency. Pour a teaspoonful on top of each marshmallow, ensuring each one is fully covered. Leave to cool for about 10 minutes.

7 Melt the chocolate in a heatproof bowl set over a pan of boiling water (don't let the base of the bowl touch the water). Alternatively, place in a microwave-safe bowl and melt in short 30-second bursts in the microwave, stirring each time to make sure it doesn't burn. Drizzle the melted chocolate over the cooled tartlets with a teaspoon and leave to set. When everything's cool, they're ready to eat.

Top Tip

To avoid getting in a sticky mess, chop marshmallows with scissors dipped in boiling water. You can put a full marshmallow in each tartlet, of course, but it's a tidier job using three-quarters of one. Don't chuck the leftover marshmallow pieces out – just stick 3 off-cuts together and you've another one sorted.

Snowballs

I'll reluctantly admit that I think these are a traditional Scottish recipe, but they have always been a firm favourite in our house. We had these as a treat on Saturdays, when Mum came home from doing the shopping in town. The bun paired with oozing raspberry jam, icing and coconut is a winning combination every time. There's a certain someone that had me smuggle these to Galway for them and later send in the post to London – that's how good they are.

MAKES 8

60g unsalted butter, softened
60g caster sugar
1 egg, lightly beaten
1 tbsp whole milk
225g self-raising flour
pinch of salt
100g Raspberry Jam (store-bought or see page 215)

For coating
120g icing sugar
a little milk, as needed
100g desiccated coconut

1 Preheat the oven to 200°C fan/220°C/gas 7. Line a baking tray with greaseproof paper.

2 Cream together the butter and caster sugar in a bowl until smooth and creamy, scraping down the sides of the bowl occasionally. Add the egg and milk, and beat until combined. Sift in the flour and salt, and mix with a spoon until combined. You can use your hand mixer at the end, if you wish, but starting with it will only result in a kitchen plastered in flour!

3 Once combined, roll the mixture into 16 balls of equal size and place on the prepared baking tray. Gently press them down to flatten the tops slightly and give a flat base.

4 Bake for about 8–10 minutes until slightly golden on top. Transfer to a wire cooling rack and leave to cool fully.

5 Match each snowball half with its closest match, then spread a layer of raspberry jam on one half and sandwich them together. Place in the fridge for about 30 minutes to help the jam firm up – this will help when dipping them.

6 In a small bowl, mix the icing sugar with a little milk until it is of a smooth, dippable/spreadable consistency. Place the desiccated coconut in a bowl next to it. Dip each snowball sandwich into the icing until coated, then dip into the desiccated coconut to cover. Place them on a wire cooling rack set over a baking tray to catch any drips. Once the excess icing has dripped off, roll them in some more desiccated coconut to ensure you have a good coating. Now get the kettle boiled and enjoy these wee balls of joy!

Melting Moments

These wee yokes are one of my Mum's go-to buns when having people around or to take visiting. They're so simple to make yet have a sophisticated look to them. They live up to their name as well by melting in your mouth. You'll be delighted with yourself when you next land round a family or friend's house with a fresh batch of these rustled up.

MAKES 14–16

225g baking margarine, softened
60g icing sugar
175g plain flour
60g cornflour

For the buttercream
125g unsalted butter, softened
225g icing sugar, sifted
¼–½ tsp vanilla extract (optional)
1 tbsp whole milk

To decorate
100g milk chocolate, melted

1 Preheat the oven to 160°C fan/180°C/gas 4. Line a baking sheet with greaseproof paper.

2 Cream together the margarine and icing sugar in a bowl until pale and fluffy, scraping the bottom and sides of your bowl to ensure it's fully combined. Sift in the flour and cornflour, and mix until fully incorporated and smooth.

3 Add the mixture to a piping bag fitted with a star nozzle and pipe 4–5cm lengths onto the prepared baking sheet, spacing them apart. Make sure they are roughly the same size, as you will be sandwiching them together.

4 Bake for about 15–20 minutes, or until a light golden colour. Remove from the oven and leave to rest on the baking sheet for a few minutes before transferring to a wire cooling rack to cool fully.

5 Meanwhile, make your buttercream by beating the softened butter until pale and creamy. Sift in the icing sugar and beat until smooth, then add the vanilla and milk, and beat once more until combined.

6 Pair your cooled biscuits to their closest match. Spread a layer of buttercream on one half, then sandwich together. Dip each end of the biscuit sandwich in the melted chocolate and place on a clean baking tray loosely covered in some greaseproof paper. Leave to set before enjoying with a cup of tea or coffee.

Apple Creams

Mum would make these when the cooking apples came into season. One of Dad's good friends, Bill, is from the Orchard County, better known as Armagh. Every September, he gives us a wooden crate full of apples and these are one of the first things to be made. They are lovely and light with a sweet tartness from the stewed apples. In my eyes, they rival a good old apple tart, which is one of my all-time favourites.

MAKES ABOUT 24

- 1 x batch of Rich Shortcrust Pastry (store-bought or see page 212)
- 3–4 Bramley apples
- 1 lemon, for squeezing
- 1 tbsp caster sugar
- 1 tsp ground cinnamon
- 2 tbsp cold water
- butter, for greasing
- plain flour, for dusting
- 50g white chocolate, melted
- 500ml double cream
- 1 tbsp icing sugar
- 1 tsp vanilla extract
- 50g milk chocolate, to decorate (optional)

Loved by Alfie

'Very tasty, very tasty.'

1. Make up a batch of your pastry (if making you own) and chill in the fridge.
2. Peel, core and chop the apples, and add to a large heavy-based pan. Add a squeeze of lemon juice, the caster sugar, ground cinnamon and cold water. Gently stew the apples over a medium heat, stirring occasionally, until they have softened and are broken down, with the odd wee chunk. Transfer to a bowl and leave to cool.
3. Meanwhile, preheat the oven to 160°C fan/180°C/gas 4 and grease 2 bun tins with butter.
4. Roll out the pastry on a lightly floured surface to about 5mm thick. With a floured 6cm pastry cutter, cut out 24 pastry shells and place the prepared bun tins. Prick a few holes in the base of each shell using a fork.
5. Bake for about 15 minutes, or until a light golden brown. Transfer to a wire cooling rack and leave to cool fully.
6. Once your pastry shells have cooled, brush a layer of melted white chocolate inside and leave to set. This will stop the stewed apple making the pastry soggy. Once the chocolate has set, fill each case with a healthy teaspoonful of stewed apple.
7. Whip the cream, icing sugar and vanilla extract together in a bowl, then either pipe swirls on top of the apple layer, or dollop a teaspoonful on top.
8. Grate over some milk chocolate, if you wish, or leave plain, and enjoy.

Top Hats

These are probably the simplest thing to make in the book and if you're from Northern Ireland, you'll know what these wee bad boys are. There isn't a child's birthday party – or any party, in fact – that is complete without Top Hats. I don't think I could count how many times I made these as a kid with my nanny and mum – they really roll back the years when I see them. Once you start making them, you'll be bringing a batch to every gathering. The only condition my nanny has for these is to use the good chocolate.

MAKES ABOUT 24–48

200–400g good-quality milk chocolate, roughly chopped
1–2 packets of marshmallows
1–2 packets of sugar-coated chocolate drops (such as Smarties)

1. Lay out 24–48 paper petit fours cases on a baking tray.
2. Melt the chocolate in a heatproof bowl set over a pan of boiling water (don't let the base of the bowl touch the water). Alternatively, place in a microwave-safe bowl and melt in short 30-second bursts in the microwave, stirring each time to make sure it doesn't burn.
3. Add a teaspoon of melted chocolate to each paper case (or even a little more, if you like – it's all down to personal preference). Pop a marshmallow on top of the chocolate and gently squeeze it down so the chocolate covers about a third of the sides of the marshmallow. Once you've got all your marshmallows in, add a little dab of chocolate on top of each one and place a sugar-coated chocolate drop on top.
4. Pop them into the fridge or somewhere cool until your chocolate has set. That's how simple these are and they're even easier to eat. If you're Northern Irish, these will transport you back to your childhood, so enjoy!

Cakes

Coffee and Walnut Cake

Coffee can be an acquired taste, but this cake is so light and subtle it's a great accompaniment to go with a cuppa for that midday pick-me-up. There's a bit of a coffee revolution at the moment, so if you have the full regalia, fire the machine up and use your preferred coffee. But don't worry – your favourite instant coffee will do the job just as well. If you don't need that caffeine hit, you can always substitute for decaf.

MAKES 1 x 20CM CAKE

175g butter, softened and cubed, plus extra for greasing
150g self-raising flour
½ tsp baking powder
½ tsp salt
175g caster sugar
3 large eggs
50ml cold espresso (or black instant coffee)
100g walnuts, plus extra to decorate

For the filling
65g unsalted butter, softened and cubed
125g icing sugar
40ml cold espresso (or black instant coffee)

For the coffee icing
100g icing sugar
20ml cold espresso (or black instant coffee)

1 Preheat the oven to 160°C fan/180°C/gas 4. Grease and line two 20cm (8in) sandwich cake tins with greaseproof paper.

2 Combine the flour, baking powder and salt in a bowl and set aside.

3 In a separate mixing bowl, beat together the butter and caster sugar until pale and fluffy, scraping the sides down halfway through.

4 Gradually add the eggs to the butter mixture, beating between each addition. Add the cold espresso and mix this in until combined.

5 If you have a food processor, you can finely blitz half of your walnuts, but don't worry if you don't. Coarsely chop, if not, and fold this half of the walnuts into the wet mixture.

6 Sift the bowl of dry ingredients into the wet ingredients and gently fold in until combined. Coarsely chop the remaining walnuts and gently fold through the batter.

7 Pour the batter evenly between the prepared cake tins.

8 Bake for about 20–25 minutes, or until lightly golden on top and an inserted skewer comes out clean. Allow the cakes to cool in the tins for 5 minutes before removing to cool fully on a wire cooling rack.

9 For the filling, beat the butter until pale and fluffy, then sift in the icing sugar and continue to beat until smooth and fluffy. Add the espresso and beat until combined.

10 Place one of your sponges on a serving plate and spread over your filling. Pop the other sponge on top of this.

11 For the coffee icing, sift the icing sugar into a bowl and add the espresso. Stir together to make a smooth icing and spread it over your cake. You can try to keep it neat at this point, but I think the rustic look of icing dripping down the sides is great. Decorate the edges with a few walnut halves or chop a few up and sprinkle over the top. Now cut yourself a big old wedge and enjoy!

Orange Loaf Cake

This recipe is one of my nanny's favourites and came from my cousin Louise. She baked one of these for my nanny many moons ago and she fell in love with it. From there on my nanny would make them on the regular. If you got one, you knew you were in the good books. It's a handy wee cake to rustle up and the orange is a refreshing addition.

MAKES 2 SMALL LOAF CAKES

225g caster sugar
170g salted butter or Stork (baking margarine)
4 eggs
285g self-raising flour, sifted
1 tsp baking powder
zest of 2 oranges plus 2 tbsp juice
100g milk chocolate, at room temperature, to decorate (optional)

For the topping
70g salted butter
170g icing sugar, sifted

1 Preheat the oven to 160°C fan/180°C/gas 4. Line two 450g (1lb) loaf tins with greaseproof paper.

2 Sift the caster sugar into a mixing bowl, add the butter and beat these together until pale and fluffy, scraping down the bottom and sides of your bowl midway through.

3 Add the eggs, flour and baking powder, along with the orange zest and juice, and mix until fully combined, scraping your bowl down midway through.

4 Divide the batter between your loaf tins (weigh them out if you must, like my my mum and nanny). Smooth these evenly with a palette knife and put a crease in the batter up the middle of each tin.

5 Bake for 45 minutes until lightly golden on top and an inserted skewer comes out clean. Remove from the oven and transfer to a wire cooling rack to cool fully.

6 Meanwhile, get stuck into making the topping. Cream the butter until pale and smooth, then gradually add the sifted icing sugar, beating between each addition. When it's nice and smooth and your cakes are cool, spread the topping over the top of each cake.

7 My nanny showed me this wee trick to decorate the tops with chocolate. Make sure your chocolate is at room temperature – slightly soft but not so much that it's melting in your hand. Use a vegetable peeler to 'peel' the end of the chocolate, giving you lovely wee curls to drop on top. It's a great tip. Get yourself a slice before some other hallion eats it all.

Mum's Victoria Sponge

Closely behind Mum's Pavlova (see page 186) is her Victoria Sponge and it comes from her little black book. This wee book is crammed with her favourite recipes she has gathered over the years. We always get one of these for our birthdays and it never lasts long. It's my best friend Clark's favourite cake – Mum made him one for his birthday once and he didn't even slice it at our house. He brought it home and ate the whole thing by himself with copious amounts of tea. If that doesn't show how good this is and makes you want to try it, I don't know what will. One more thing to twist your arm . . . it's an all-in-one method, so it's ridiculously simple. Does that seal the deal?

MAKES 1 x 20CM CAKE

For the sponge
225g butter, softened, or Stork (baking margarine), plus extra for greasing
225g self-raising flour, plus extra for dusting
225g caster sugar
4 eggs

For the buttercream
115g butter, softened
225g icing sugar, sifted
1 tsp vanilla extract
small amount of milk, if needed

Raspberry Jam (store-bought or see page 215)
icing sugar, for dusting

1. Preheat the oven to 160°C fan/180°C/gas 4 and grease and line the base of two 20cm (8in) sandwich cake tins with greaseproof paper and dust the sides with some flour.
2. Sift the flour into a mixing bowl, then add the caster sugar, butter and eggs. Begin to beat this on a low speed, then gradually increase the speed. You want everything to combine and become smooth. Midway through, scrape the bottom of the bowl to make sure everything is getting mixed together.
3. Once you get a nice smooth batter, divide it equally between the cake tins. You can get particular like my mum and weigh it out if you'd like. Smooth it out and create a small divot in the middle – this stops it from rising too much in the centre.
4. Bake for 40–45 minutes until golden on top and an inserted skewer comes out clean. Remove your sponges from their tins and allow them to cool fully on a wire cooling rack.
5. For the buttercream, beat the butter until it's pale and fluffy – this can take about 5 minutes. My mum would always do this in a tall measuring jug with an electric hand mixer. She always says it makes the butter fluffier and smoother. Gradually add the sifted icing sugar to this, mixing well between each addition. Finally, add the vanilla extract and mix through. If you find it a little thick at this point, add a little milk to thin it out to a spreadable but holding consistency.

Loved by Alfie

'I taught your mum everything she knows!'

6 Spread a layer of raspberry jam on the inside base of your sponges. You can either pipe or spread the buttercream on what will be the bottom sponge of your cake. Piping is a better option, as the jam doesn't run or mix with the buttercream. Pop the other sponge, jam-side down, onto your buttercream layer and gently press it down. Finally, give it a little dusting of icing sugar. Now slice 'er up and get the kettle on. There is no better combo than a big wedge of this and a bucket of tae. You can ask my mate Clark!

Sticky Ginger Loaf Cake

We always had one of these in the cupboard, not sure why. Maybe for when someone came round for a cuppa tae, but I always loved a slice with some butter. It's lightly spiced and lovely and moist. I've seen my dad polish off one of these by himself. You're probably thinking we are complete hallions here, just inhaling anything in our path! But when you make something good, well, it's hard to stop yourself.

MAKES 1 LARGE LOAF CAKE

100g butter
100g golden syrup
140g treacle
100g soft dark brown sugar
200g plain flour
1 tsp bicarbonate of soda
1 tbsp ground ginger
1 tsp ground cinnamon
1 tsp ground nutmeg
50g crystallised ginger
2 eggs
80ml milk

1. Preheat the oven to 160°C fan/180°C/gas 4 and line a 900g (2lb) loaf tin with greaseproof paper.
2. Gently melt the butter, golden syrup, treacle and dark soft brown sugar in a small pan over a low–medium heat. Set aside once melted.
3. Sift the flour into a large bowl along with the bicarbonate of soda, ginger, cinnamon and nutmeg.
4. Make a well in the middle of the dry ingredients and pour in the slightly cooled melted ingredients. Mix with a spoon or spatula until fully combined and smooth, then add the crystallised ginger.
5. In a small bowl, whisk together the eggs and milk, then pour this into the batter. Stir well until fully combined, then pour into your loaf tin.
6. Bake for about 45 minutes, or until an inserted skewer comes out clean. Allow to cool in the tin for 10 minutes, then transfer to a wire cooling rack to cool fully.
7. You can get stuck in straight away, plastering it in real butter. But if you wrap it tightly in some kitchen foil and pop it in an airtight container, the flavours will develop over a few days. It might be a good idea to make two cakes. One to keep you going and the other to look forward to, unless someone lands unannounced for a cuppa tae.

Nanny's Boiled Fruit Cake

I feel like this recipe is a forgotten classic. One of the many reasons I love baking is to learn these wonderful recipes from days gone by, because they really are special. I think this one lacks the love it deserves because it seems like an 'old person's' cake. Nothing against old people – I love them and people think my grandparents are cooler than me, so I can't talk. People automatically think dried fruit isn't going to be nice, but once you boil everything up it becomes so plump and delicious. There are few better things that come out of an oven, I tell ye.

MAKES 2 SMALL LOAF CAKES

170g butter
140g caster sugar
1 x 227g tin of crushed/chopped pineapple (including the juice)
340g mixed dried fruit (such as sultanas and raisins)
85ml water
240g plain flour
1 tsp bicarbonate of soda
2 tsp mixed spice
2 tsp ground cinnamon
2 eggs

1. Preheat the oven to 140°C fan/160°C/gas 3. Line two 450g (1lb) loaf tins with greaseproof paper.
2. Add the butter, caster sugar and crushed pineapple to a saucepan, along with the dried fruit and water. Bring to the boil, then simmer for about 10–15 minutes, stirring occasionally. The mixture will start to darken in colour and thicken up. At this point, set it aside and leave to cool.
3. Sift the flour into a large bowl along with the bicarbonate of soda, mixed spice and cinnamon. Mix with a whisk so everything is evenly distributed.
4. In a separate bowl, lightly beat the eggs.
5. Once the boiled mixture has cooled to about room temperature, gradually add the beaten eggs and dry ingredients to it. Gently fold together between each addition. Once you have it all combined, divide between your loaf tins. As usual, you can weigh them up if you're pernickety (like everyone in my family). Smooth the tops with the back of a spoon or palette knife.
6. Bake for about 1 hour, or until golden on top and an inserted skewer comes out clean. Allow them to cool fully in the tins, because they're very moist and delicate when cut, especially when warm. These yokes are moist enough without butter, but there's no better combo when you lather it in some real butter.

Loved by Alfie

'It's that moist you wouldn't need butter.'

Chocolate Fudge Cake

This one is for all the chocolate lovers out there. I had to include this recipe because of one of my best friends, Kyle. He gave up chocolate for 18 years and I rustled this up for him to ease him back into it. It's a proper moist and fudgy chocolate cake, none of this crumbly, dry carry on. It's a sight to behold. This makes a decent-sized cake that will easily feed a large party or gathering, so if you want to halve the recipe, go for it.

MAKES 1 x 20CM 4-LAYER CAKE

400g butter, cubed, plus extra for greasing
250ml cold water
2 tbsp instant coffee granules
400g dark chocolate (about 60% cocoa solids), chopped
400g caster sugar
400g soft light brown sugar
½ tsp bicarbonate of soda
50g cocoa powder
170g self-raising flour
170g plain flour
6 eggs
150ml buttermilk

For the chocolate ganache
500g dark chocolate (about 60% cocoa solids), chopped
750ml double cream
5 tbsp caster sugar

1 Preheat the oven to 140°C fan/160°C/gas 3 and grease and line four 20cm (8in) sandwich cake tins (two tins if you're halving the recipe).

2 Place the water in a heatproof bowl and mix in the coffee granules, then add the butter and chocolate and place over a saucepan of boiling water (do not let the bowl touch the surface of the water). Gently melt over a medium–low heat, stirring occasionally. Set aside to cool when melted.

3 In a separate large mixing bowl, combine the caster sugar, light brown sugar, bicarbonate of soda, cocoa powder and both flours. Run this through your hands to squash out any lumps.

4 In a separate bowl, beat the eggs and buttermilk together until they froth up nicely. Add the cooled chocolate mixture and egg mixture to the dry ingredients, folding together until smooth. It will give you a rich and thick batter.

5 Pour the batter evenly into your cake tins. You can weigh these up if you'd like to ensure they are even.

6 Bake for about 50 minutes–1 hour, or until a skewer comes out clean. This might vary for each sponge as ovens can vary in temperature as well as the position of each sponge. Allow them to cool in the tins and then turn out onto a wire cooling rack, removing your greaseproof paper.

7 For the ganache, add the chocolate to a large bowl. Heat the cream and sugar in a small pan until just before it boils, then pour this over the chocolate and mix until melted and smooth. Allow this to cool until it forms a nice thick, but spreadable, ganache. You can speed this up by popping it in the fridge or freezer, but be sure to keep an eye on it and stir every 15 minutes or so.

8 Place a sponge on a serving plate or cake board and begin construction. Spread a layer of ganache on top of the base sponge, then place another sponge on top. Repeat until you've used all your sponges. Spread some ganache on the sides and top of the cake and smooth it out. It doesn't have to be fancy and you can put your own spin on the design. Once I have the ganache roughly smooth, I dip a teaspoon into some boiling water and press the back of it into the cake, pulling it around to create a spiralling indent. But do what you feel like. If it's messy, don't worry – it's all about the taste.

9 Now you can slice it up and enjoy! I like to blast it in the microwave for about 15–30 seconds and serve with a big scoop of vanilla ice cream. It truly is magical.

Loved by Alfie

'It's like something you'd get in one of those high-end restaurants.'

Madeira Cake

You might have heard the yarn about the bakery where everything was £1, except for one wee cake, which was £2. When asked why, the baker said 'That's madeira (m' dearer) cake'. It's a horrendous joke, but this wee cake definitely isn't. It looks unassuming and plain, but it's delicious with hints of lemon and vanilla. Pair it with some homemade custard and you will have a rush of nostalgia taking you back to your childhood.

MAKES 1 x 18CM CAKE

- 115g unsalted butter, softened, plus extra for greasing
- 140g caster sugar
- zest of 1 lemon
- 225g self-raising flour
- 2 eggs, lightly beaten
- ¼ tsp salt
- a few drops of vanilla extract
- 2–3 tbsp milk

1. Preheat the oven to 160°C fan/180°C/gas 4. Grease and line a 18cm (7in) cake tin with greaseproof paper.
2. In a large mixing bowl, cream together the butter and sugar. Give the sides of your bowl a scrape down halfway through and continue to beat until pale and fluffy.
3. Add the lemon zest, flour, eggs, salt, vanilla and milk. Slowly beat until everything is combined and your cake batter is smooth.
4. Pour the batter into the prepared cake tin and smooth out the top. Bake for about 55 minutes–1 hour, or until firm to the touch and an inserted skewer comes out clean.
5. Allow to cool in the tin for about 10 minutes before removing to a wire cooling rack. It's best to let it cool fully before slicing due to it being so soft and delicate. But once it's sliceable, tear away and lather in some real butter, or fresh custard if you're treating yourself.

Carrot Cake

This classic eluded me for years because I thought carrots in a cake should never be a thing. But once I got a taste many years ago there was no looking back. This version is so simple, you can even make it without the fancy equipment, just your trusty old whisk. It locks in all the moisture and has the creamiest cheese frosting, with pecans for added texture. If you're contemplating making a cake, just remember this one is full of carrots, so it's basically healthy if you ask me.

MAKES 1 x 23CM CAKE

- 295ml vegetable oil, plus extra for greasing
- 260g plain flour
- 2 tsp bicarbonate of soda
- ½ tsp fine sea salt
- 1½ tsp ground cinnamon
- 1 tsp mixed spice (optional)
- 200g caster sugar
- 190g soft light brown sugar
- 1 tsp vanilla extract
- 4 large eggs, at room temperature
- 300g carrots, peeled and grated
- 65g raisins
- 150g pecans, coarsely chopped
- Cream Cheese Frosting (see page 216), to decorate

1. Preheat the oven to 160°C fan/180°C/gas 4. Grease and line two 23cm (9in) cake tins with greaseproof paper.
2. Combine the flour, bicarbonate of soda, salt, ground cinnamon and mixed spice (if using) in a bowl and whisk to mix.
3. In a separate large bowl, whisk together the vegetable oil, caster sugar, soft brown sugar and vanilla extract. Gradually add the eggs, whisking well between each addition until you have a smooth mixture.
4. Gradually add the dry ingredients, folding them in with a spatula. Once combined, add the carrots, raisins and two-thirds of the pecans, folding them throughout.
5. Pour the batter equally between your prepared tins.
6. Bake for about 35–40 minutes, or until an inserted skewer comes out clean. Allow the sponges to cool in the tins for 15 minutes before removing to a wire cooling rack to cool fully.
7. To make it easier to ice, you can cut off the little mound that generally rises in the middle of each sponge (bonus: you can have a wee taste before anyone else). Spread a layer of cream cheese frosting on the base sponge and sandwich the other sponge on top. Spread another layer of cream cheese on the top and sprinkle with the remaining chopped pecans. This cake is so moist, I'd hazard saying you won't need a cup of tea with it. But not enjoying this with a cuppa would just be cruel.

Lemon Drizzle Cupcakes

These wee lemon drizzle cupcakes are a delicious treat, especially if you're a fan of citrus flavours. It's basically my lemon drizzle cake recipe scaled down so you don't have an overwhelming amount of cupcakes. Then again, you might scale it back up to make more once you try it. The extra additions of a smooth buttercream with melted white chocolate and the delicious lemon topping are something I might have to adopt in the original recipe.

MAKES 12

150g unsalted butter, softened
150g caster sugar
3 eggs, lightly beaten
150g self-raising flour
zest of 1 lemon

For the drizzle
40g caster sugar
juice of 1 lemon

For the buttercream
200g unsalted butter, softened
400g icing sugar
2 tsp melted white chocolate

To decorate
150g lemon curd
extra lemon zest (optional)

1 Preheat the oven to 180°C fan/200°C/gas 6.

2 Cream the butter and sugar together in a mixing bowl until pale and fluffy. Add the eggs and gently beat these into the mix until combined. Don't worry if the mixture curdles slightly, it will come together once you add the rest of the ingredients. Add the flour and gently beat this in until smooth. Finally, add the lemon zest and mix in. You can do this in a stand mixer or by hand – just ensure your ingredients are well combined.

3 Pop 12 cupcake cases into a cupcake tin and spoon an equal amount of the batter into each case. My nanny would use an ice cream scoop for this – it's so handy if you have one.

4 Bake for about 15 minutes until they are golden and spring back when touched.

5 While the cakes are in the oven, make the drizzle. Combine the caster sugar and lemon juice in a bowl and mix until dissolved.

6 When you remove the cakes from the oven, spoon the lemon drizzle equally over each one. Allow them to cool in the tin for a few minutes, before transferring to a wire cooling rack to cool fully.

7 Meanwhile, make the buttercream. Beat the butter in a bowl until pale and smooth. Gradually sift in the icing sugar, beating between each addition until fully combined and smooth. Add the melted white chocolate and beat in.

8 Once your cupcakes have cooled, pipe swirls of buttercream on top and drizzle with some lemon curd to finish. If you're a real lemon lover, you could also grate some more lemon zest on top. These are a nice change from a normal lemon drizzle cake and potentially tastier with the additions on top.

Nanny's Light Sponge with Cream and Fruit

This sponge surprisingly doesn't use any butter and it's the reason for it being so light. You will feel like you're eating a cloud with this one. The fact that it isn't dense means you can polish off a few slices without any guilt or hesitation. It's a perfect afternoon treat on a sunny day and a great way to use up those seasonal fruits we are blessed with.

MAKES 1 x 20CM CAKE

- 5 large eggs
- 140g caster sugar
- 140g self-raising flour
- 250ml double cream, whipped
- 2 tbsp icing sugar, plus extra for dusting
- 1 punnet of fresh strawberries and raspberries

Loved by Alfie

'Like eating a cloud!'

1. Preheat the oven to 180°C fan/200°C/gas 6. Line two 20cm (8in) cake tins with greaseproof paper.
2. In a large mixing bowl, whisk the eggs with the sugar at a slow pace to begin with, then after a few minutes gradually build up to full speed. The mixture will start to lighten in colour and grow in volume. This will take around 5 minutes and you will know it's done when you lift your whisk and the mixture leaves a trail.
3. Gradually sift the flour into your mixture, folding in gently with your whisk attachment between each addition. Make sure to be gentle at this point to avoid knocking the air out of the mixture. Use a spatula at the end to scrape the bottom of the bowl, to ensure everything is fully incorporated.
4. Pour the batter evenly between the prepared cake tins and bake for about 15–20 minutes until golden brown on top and an inserted skewer comes out clean. Allow to cool in the tins for about 5 minutes before removing to a wire cooling rack to cool fully.
5. Whip the cream and icing sugar together when you're ready to decorate. Carefully slice each sponge in half and spread the bottom layer with half of the cream. (You can also spread a layer of jam on the base prior to adding the cream, but that's all down to preference.) Sandwich your sponge back together and top with another layer of cream. Chop the strawberries in any way you'd like and arrange on top along with the raspberries. Dust the top with some icing sugar, then dig into your beautifully light sponge fit for any occasion.

Buttermilk Fruit Loaf Cake

This recipe came from my auntie Heather and is loved by me and Nanny. This recipe makes three small loaf cakes, so it's a perfect wee treat to have on hand for that afternoon cup of tea or visitor calling in, or if you're feeling generous to take to someone's house as an unannounced gift. It has a lovely delicate texture and flavour and is packed full of juicy fruit. The words my Granda Alfie used were: 'that has it, yes'. Make what you want from that, but the cake was gone in no time, so you know it's good. You can also bake this in a 23cm (9in) cake tin, but the timings will differ.

MAKES 3 SMALL LOAF CAKES

450g plain flour
170g salted butter, cubed
170g caster sugar
1 tsp bicarbonate of soda
2 tsp mixed spice
450g mixed dried fruit (such as sultanas and raisins)
55g mixed peel (optional)
3 eggs, beaten
about 450ml buttermilk

1. Preheat the oven to 160°C fan/180°C/gas 4. Line three 450g (1lb) loaf tins with greaseproof paper.
2. Sift the flour into a large mixing bowl and add the butter. Work the butter into the flour, rubbing it through your fingertips until it resembles breadcrumbs. You will know it's combined enough when there are no big lumps left.
3. Add the sugar, bicarbonate of soda and mixed spice, and work this through the flour and butter. Add the mixed fruit and mixed peel, and stir until evenly distributed.
4. Add the beaten eggs and combine, then gradually add the buttermilk mixing it in until you have a nice dropping consistency.
5. Divide the batter among the prepared tins and smooth the tops.
6. Bake for about 45 minutes until lightly golden on top and an inserted skewer comes out clean.
7. Allow the cakes to cool in their tins for about 30 minutes before removing to a wire cooling rack and cooling fully. Now slice up and eat as is, or lather with some real butter, alongside a fresh cup of tea.

Black Forest Gâteau

I remember running around Galway with Nanny and Granda looking for kirsch, just so Nanny could make this. Trust me, it was well worth the hassle. I always argued that chocolate cake and fruit shouldn't mix, but when I had this I admitted I was wrong. Moral of the story – don't knock it until you've tried it.

MAKES 1 x 20–23CM CAKE

4 eggs, lightly beaten
100g caster sugar
75g self-raising flour
35g cocoa powder

For the filling and topping
2 x 420g tins/jars of black cherries in juice
2 tbsp cornflour
3–4 tbsp kirsch (cherry liqueur)
600ml double cream, whipped
50g toasted flaked almonds
100g dark chocolate

Loved by Alfie

'Don't get enough of this!'

1 Preheat the oven to 160°C fan/180°C/gas 4. Line the base and sides of two 20–23cm (8–9in) round cake tins.

2 Add the eggs and sugar to a large mixing bowl or stand mixer and whisk on a high speed until pale and thick. Sift in the flour and cocoa powder and gently fold throughout, avoiding knocking the air out.

3 Divide the batter equally between the two tins, gently smoothing the tops.

4 Bake for 20–25 minutes until well risen, springing back when gently pressed and shrinking from the sides of the tins. Turn these out onto a wire cooling rack and leave to cool fully.

5 Drain the tins of black cherries and reserve the juice. Save about 8 cherries to use as decoration and de-stone the rest.

6 Add the cornflour to a saucepan set over a medium–high heat and gradually add the reserved cherry juice, stirring until it starts to thicken and come to the boil. Reduce to a simmer and cook for a further 2 minutes. Remove from the heat and leave to cool.

7 When the cherry syrup is cool, add the stoned cherries and kirsch, and stir to combine.

8 You can slice your cooled sponges in half to create more layers, but I like to use them just as they are. Sandwich your cake layers with half of the whipped cream (you can pipe this on if you wish) and all of the cherry mixture. Spread (or pipe) the remaining cream on top of the sponges. Sprinkle with the toasted flaked almonds and pop your saved cherries on top of the cream swirls. Grate the chocolate over the top or use a vegetable peeler to create chocolate curls for decorating. Now slice yourself a big wedge and enjoy this light but decadent dessert.

Peach Upside-Down Cake

I always thought these cakes were daunting to make – I was wrong. This may look fancy, but you can whip it up on a whim. It looks the part and tastes even better, with its caramelised peaches and tender, flavoursome sponge. It's perfect for a summer dessert and pairs beautifully with some ice cream or even a lathering of custard.

MAKES 1 x 23CM CAKE

4–5 peaches
170g caster sugar
2 tbsp water

For the wet ingredients
225g caster sugar
100g soft light brown sugar
120ml olive oil
115g unsalted butter, melted
2 large eggs
175ml buttermilk
1 tsp vanilla extract
½ tsp almond extract

For the dry ingredients
240g plain flour
2 tsp salt
½ tsp bicarbonate of soda
½ tsp baking powder

1 Preheat the oven to 160°C fan/180°C/gas 4. Line the base of a 23cm (9in) cake tin with greaseproof paper.

2 Cut the peaches in half and remove the stones. Finely slice each half and fan the slices around the lined tin, making sure to fill any gaps.

3 Add the caster sugar and water to a saucepan and set over a medium heat. Stay with this, as it can easily burn. It will start to caramelise and become amber in colour. It can be tempting to stir this when little chunks of sugar clump together, but avoid this. Instead, swirl your saucepan around on the hob allowing it to combine and caramelise. This can take about 5 minutes. When it forms an amber caramel, pour this over the peaches in the tin.

4 Add the caster sugar, soft light brown sugar, olive oil, melted butter and eggs to a large mixing bowl. Whisk until smooth, then add the buttermilk and whisk until combined. Add the vanilla and almond extracts, then whisk again.

5 In a separate bowl, add all the dry ingredients, giving them a quick stir to combine. Sift this into your wet ingredients and gently fold in until smooth and combined. Pour the batter over the caramelised peaches.

6 Bake for about 1 hour until golden brown on top and an inserted skewer comes out clean. Allow to cool in the tin for 15 minutes.

7 Run a knife around the edge of the tin to loosen the cake. Place your serving plate on top and flip the cake upside down onto the plate. Remove the tin and peel off your greaseproof paper. You can allow it to cool fully before serving, but it's dreamy when slightly warm with a scoop of vanilla ice cream!

Haystacks

This is my auntie Marnie's speciality and my dad could polish off a full slab of it himself, that's no lie. It's a simple one to make and look at, but there's something about it that makes it so moreish – especially when you douse it in homemade Vanilla Custard (see page 217) or even better slice in half and fill with fresh cream. My auntie normally just bakes from the feel and look of this, so it was a mission getting this recipe off her. Also, my dad insists hers tastes better simply because she has her own hens and gets fresh eggs every day, which I have to agree with.

MAKES ABOUT 16 SQUARES

280g salted butter, softened
280g caster sugar
5 large eggs, lightly beaten
280g self-raising flour, sifted
dash of vanilla extract (optional)
½ jar of Raspberry Jam (store-bought or see page 215)
200g desiccated coconut

Optional filling
250ml double cream
2 tbsp icing sugar

1 Preheat the oven to 140°C fan/160°C/gas 3. Line a deep, 30 x 23cm (12 x 9in) baking tin with greaseproof paper.

2 In a mixing bowl, cream the butter and sugar together on a medium speed until pale and smooth. You will have to scrape the sides down a few times to ensure it's fully combined. Add a little egg and then a few tablespoons of the flour, mixing until combined. Repeat this process until you've used both up and the mixture is smooth. Add the vanilla and mix in well.

3 Pour your mixture into the prepared tin and bake for about 35–40 minutes, or until golden on top and an inserted skewer comes out clean.

4 Allow the sponge to cool in the tin for about 15 minutes before turning out onto a wire cooling rack and leaving it to cool fully.

5 Once cooled, there are two ways of decorating:

Either heat the jam in a saucepan until spreadable, then spread it evenly across the top of and sides of your sponge. Plaster the whole of the sponge with the desiccated coconut and then slice and enjoy with a cup of tea or swimming in some vanilla custard.

Alternatively, you can slice the sponge lengthways to create two separate layers. Whip the double cream with the icing sugar, then spread this on one half and sandwich the other on top. Now spread your heated jam on the top sponge, allowing it to drip down the sides and partially onto the bottom layer, before covering in the desiccated coconut.

Traybakes

Fifteens

The Northern Irish take pride in their traybakes – and Fifteens sit at the top of the list of the best (even though they're not baked – in Northern Ireland, we'd still call it a traybake!). My teammates loved them so much I used to make them every Tuesday for the coffee room as a bit of a morale boost during the winter months. They're traditionally made with glacé cherries, but my mate Carey doesn't like cherries, so the Chocolate Fifteen was born. I've given you both options here. Fifteens are called that because you are supposed to put fifteen of each main ingredient in, but they were made back in the day when you could buy very small tins of condensed milk. They only sell large tins now, so these are actually Thirties! You'll not complain because you'll get more of them.

MAKES ABOUT 30

30 digestive biscuits
30 marshmallows, chopped
30 glacé cherries or 150–200g milk chocolate (or half milk and half white chocolate)
1 x 397g tin of condensed milk
about 100g desiccated coconut, for sprinkling

1. Blitz the digestives in a food processor until finely ground, or you can go old school and use a rolling pin and a ziplock bag. Place in a large bowl.
2. Boil the kettle and pour out a mug of hot water. Dip a pair of scissors or a knife into the hot water and use to chop the marshmallows in half. The hot water stops everything getting sticky. Add to the bowl along with the digestive crumbs and mix well.
3. Do the same with the glacé cherries (if using). Alternatively, chop up the chocolate and throw it in.
4. Pour in the tin of condensed milk and mix with a wooden spoon until well combined and there are no dry bits left.
5. Cut a large sheet of kitchen foil and lay it on your work surface. Sprinkle half of the desiccated coconut over the foil. Take half of the mixture and drop it into the desiccated coconut, then roll it into a thick sausage shape. I'll always say the thicker the better, but it's all down to preference. Once it's nicely rolled and completely covered in desiccated coconut, wrap it up tightly in the kitchen foil. Repeat with the other half of the mixture and desiccated coconut.
6. Leave to set for about 30 minutes. You can pop them into the fridge, but I much prefer them moist and squidgy.
7. Unwrap and chop each log into about 15 thick slices, then try what is one of the greatest gifts Northern Ireland has given to the world – more iconic and better than Georgie Best, Alex Higgins and Rory McIlroy combined! They'll keep for up to 4–5 days in a sealed container.

Loved by Alfie

'A classic.'

Rocky Roads

These might be my little sister Emma's favourite treat. Every time I rustled a batch up for an occasion it was on the condition I made extra for her. She still brings them to her old job every so often, even though she left years ago. They're also a great way to use up any leftover chocolate from Christmas or Easter. People will joke that they don't know what leftover chocolate is, but we all have it at times. They squarely hit the spot, that's for sure.

MAKES ABOUT 16

- 400g milk chocolate, broken up
- 270g butter, cubed
- 4–6 tbsp golden syrup
- 400g digestive biscuits
- 200g marshmallows, chopped
- 100g nuts of choice, chopped
- 150–200g chocolate sweets of choice (leftover Christmas and Easter chocolates work great)

To decorate

- 150g milk chocolate
- mini marshmallows
- extra chocolate sweets
- 50g white chocolate, chopped

1. Combine the milk chocolate, butter and golden syrup in a heavy-based saucepan and gently melt over a low–medium heat. Leave to cool.
2. Finely crush half of the digestives in a food processor or in a bowl with a rolling pin. Roughly crush the other half with your hands so it's not all like dust. Make sure to use a big bowl for this. Add the chopped marshmallows and give these mix so they don't clump into one big pile. Add the chopped nuts along with your chocolate sweets. Pour in the cooled chocolate mixture and mix it all together until combined.
3. Line a 25 x 20cm (10 x 8in) baking tin with some greaseproof paper or a few strips of cling film, as that makes it easy to slip the traybake out. Transfer the mixture to the tin and press it out to fill any gaps. Don't worry if it's not completely flat. Place in a cool spot or the fridge until it firms up.
4. To decorate, melt the milk chocolate over a bain-marie or in 30-second bursts in the microwave. Spread this evenly over the top of the rocky road and sprinkle over some mini marshmallows along with some extra chocolate sweets. Melt down the white chocolate in the same way and drizzle this over the top. Leave to set.
5. Slice into your desired portions and eat with a cuppa tae.

Loved by Alfie

'Tasty with a cuppa tae.'

Diana Bars

These are very similar to Fifteens (see page 113), but at the same time so different. They're like a Fifteen's good-lookin' cousin. These are really only known in Northern Ireland – we seem to have the run on the traybake game for some reason. Like all my recipes, they're simple to make – honestly, I think anyone could rustle them up. They're sweet, but seriously delicious with their coconutty, chewy marshmallow and crunchy biscuit texture.

MAKES ABOUT 12

225g rich tea biscuits, crushed
150g marshmallows, chopped
115g butter
1 x 397g tin of condensed milk
115g desiccated coconut

To decorate
200g white chocolate, melted
50–100g mini marshmallows (or regular ones, chopped)

1 Blitz the rich tea biscuits up in a food processor or bash the life out of them with a rolling pin in a bowl to get the same result. You can hold a few back and break them up with your hands if you like a few chunkier, crunchy bits. Pop into a larger bowl, add the marshmallows and mix, so the marshmallows don't clump together.

2 Add the butter to a saucepan and gently melt it down over a low heat. Add the condensed milk and mix until combined, then add the desiccated coconut, stirring it through. Add to the bowl with the dry ingredients and combine using a wooden spoon.

3 Tip the mixture into a 26 x 20cm (10 x 8in) baking tin lined with some greaseproof paper and roughly even the top out with a spoon or palette knife.

4 Pour the melted white chocolate over the top and smooth it over, then scatter with the mini marshmallows (I recommend the mini ones – they're just handier).

5 Leave to set in the fridge for a few hours before slicing it up. As always, the only thing left to do is wet the cup and enjoy!

Nutty Brownies

Some will disagree, but I think a brownie should be moist and gooey. If you like them that way, you'll love these yokes. If not, I think you might be converted after trying them. They are so moist and decadent, and the nuts are the perfect change up in texture. With a cuppa tae or a coffee, it really is a winning combination.

MAKES ABOUT 12

150g salted butter
150g dark chocolate
150g caster sugar
150g soft light brown sugar
3 eggs
75g plain flour
30g cocoa powder
½ tsp ground cinnamon
½ tsp salt
100g white chocolate, chopped
150g nuts of choice (pecans, walnuts, pistachios, etc.), chopped

Optional decoration
melted milk and white chocolate, for drizzling

1. Preheat the oven to 160°C fan/180°C/gas 4. Line a 20cm (8in) square baking tin with greaseproof paper.
2. Add the butter and chocolate to a bain-marie and gently melt down over a medium heat, stirring occasionally. Alternatively, you can do this in the microwave in 30-second blasts, stirring in between. Once melted, set aside and allow to cool.
3. Pop both sugars into a mixing bowl along with the eggs and whisk for about 5 minutes until nice and fluffy. Once your chocolate mixture is cool, add to the sugar and egg mixture and gently fold together until combined.
4. Sift in the flour, cocoa powder, cinnamon and salt, and gently fold until combined.
5. Add the chopped white chocolate along with half of the nuts, mixing these throughout.
6. Pour the mixture into your prepared tin and bake for 20 minutes.
7. Remove from the oven and add the rest of the nuts on top, gently pressing them in. Pop back into the oven for a further 10 minutes, then remove and allow to cool fully in the tin. These are extremely moist and gooey, so make sure to let them fully set. You can pop them into the fridge after an hour or so to speed up the process.
8. When set, drizzle with some melted milk and white chocolate, if you fancy it, then slice up and enjoy!

Chocolate Tiffin

Tiffin seems to be something we all love but rarely make. I always thought of it as a rocky road for adults, but it's too tasty not to be for everyone. With a rich, chocolatey flavour, loads of texture from the biscuit and nuts, and the slight chew from the dried fruit, it's a super-easy traybake and one you'll make regularly once you try it.

MAKES ABOUT 12

140g salted butter
200g milk chocolate with hazelnuts
4 tbsp golden syrup
280g digestive biscuits
50g cocoa powder
60g pistachios
60g sultanas
30g raisins
100–200g milk chocolate, chopped, for topping

1 Add the butter, hazelnut chocolate and golden syrup to a saucepan and gently melt down over a medium-low heat, stirring occasionally. Once melted, set aside to slightly cool.

2 Partially blitz the digestives in a food processor or crush them up in a bowl. You want half finely crushed and the rest in small bits to add some crunch. Add these to a large mixing bowl, sift in the cocoa powder, add the pistachios, sultanas and raisins, and mix well.

3 Pour in the cooled chocolate mixture and combine everything with a wooden spoon.

4 Tip the mixture into a 20cm (8in) square baking tin lined with some greaseproof paper, pressing it down firmly. Place it into the fridge for about an hour to firm up slightly.

5 Melt the chocolate for topping over a bain-marie or in 30-second bursts in the microwave, then pour it over the cooled base. Spread it out evenly and run a skewer through it to make a feathered pattern.

6 Place it back in the fridge for an hour or so until the chocolate has set.

7 Remove from the tin and slice it into portions. Enjoy!

Currant Squares

Currant squares, fruit slices, flies' graveyards or fly pie . . . the names for these go on and on. I've always known them as currant squares and they're one of my favourite traditional recipes. If you like mince pies, these are an acceptable alternative to have all year round (so people don't think you're odd). Plus, I think these taste better.

MAKES ABOUT 24

340g sultanas, destalked
60g dried apricots, chopped
1 Bramley apple, peeled, cored and chopped into small chunks
170g caster sugar, plus extra for dusting
180ml water
2 tbsp cornflour mixed with a little water
1½ tsp ground cinnamon
1½ tsp mixed spice
plain flour, for dusting
2 x batches of Shortcrust Pastry (store-bought or see page 212)

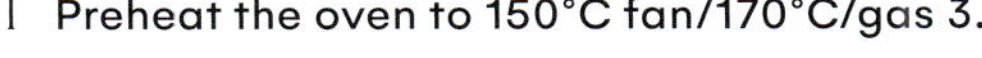

1. Preheat the oven to 150°C fan/170°C/gas 3.
2. Add the sultanas, dried apricots, apple, sugar and water to a saucepan, bring to the boil, then lightly simmer for about 10 minutes, stirring continuously. After a few minutes of simmering, gradually add your cornflour mix. It will start to reduce and thicken up nicely. Nearing the end of the simmering time, add the cinnamon and mixed spice, and mix well. Set aside to cool fully.
3. On a lightly floured work surface, roll out the first batch of pastry to about 5mm thick and just larger than a deep 23 x 33cm (9 x 13in) baking tray. Roll this into the baking tray, covering the base and edges. Gently press the pastry in at the edges. Don't worry if there's the odd hole – you can patch these up. Trim off any excess pastry.
4. Tip the fruit mixture on top of the pastry base and smooth it out.
5. Roll out the other batch of pastry in the same fashion and roll it over the top like a lid. Gently seal the edges with your fingertips and trim any excess pastry off with a knife, then press all around the edges with the back of a fork to seal. Prick the top of the pastry all over with a fork to allow steam to escape.
6. Bake for about 40–45 minutes until lightly golden on top.
7. Remove from the oven, sprinkle over a decent amount of caster sugar and allow to cool before slicing. These are a true classic in my eyes and will always transport me back to my nanny's kitchen when I settle into one with a cuppa tae.

Loved by Alfie

'They're just nice!'

Caramel Squares

You might know these as millionaire's shortbread but I always call them caramel squares. I remember helping to make these all the time at Nanny's as a young fella and now I'm rustling them up myself. My mum is a big fan of them but will always compare any she has to Nanny's recipe. These are my best mate Carey's favourite traybake. When I went over with a squad of our mates to watch his Premiership Rugby debut, he insisted that I make him a batch and I smuggled them over on the flight. We arrived the night before the match. He inhaled a few straight away, started the next day off with two more, and had a few more on the way to the game. If that's not carb loading in style, I don't know what is!

MAKES ABOUT 24

For the shortbread base
255g plain flour, sifted
170g salted butter, softened
85g caster sugar

For the caramel
120g salted butter
60g caster sugar
2 tbsp golden syrup
1 x 397g tin of condensed milk

For the topping
250–300g milk chocolate, melted
100g white chocolate, melted

1 Preheat the oven to 150°C fan/170°C/gas 3.

2 For the base, add the flour and butter to a food processor and blitz until it starts to come together. You can also do this by hand – rub the butter through the flour with your fingertips until it's fully combined. Now add the caster sugar and blitz until it looks like clumpy breadcrumbs. Run it through your hands to make sure it's fully combined.

3 Tip the mixture into a 20 x 25cm (8 x 10in) baking tin and press to cover the base, smoothing it out with a palette knife.

4 Bake for 20–25 minutes until slightly golden on top and evenly cooked. Keep an eye on it. When it's ready, leave to cool.

5 Meanwhile, make the caramel. In a heavy-based pan, combine the butter, caster sugar, golden syrup and condensed milk. Melt these down over a medium heat. When melted, bring to the boil, then simmer for about 5–8 minutes, stirring continuously so it doesn't stick to the pan, until it thickens into a nice golden caramel.

6 Pour the caramel over the base and smooth it out using a palette knife. Allow to cool for about 45 minutes–1 hour.

7 For the topping, melt the milk chocolate over a bain-marie or in short 30-second bursts in the microwave. I find it best to use the bain-marie. Pour this over your caramel and smooth it out evenly.

8 Melt the white chocolate in the same way. You can either drizzle stripes of this across the milk chocolate using a teaspoon or fill a small piping bag and pipe it on for a better finish. Feather the stripes with a skewer or toothpick by running it up and down through both chocolates.

9 Allow to firm up in a cool spot or the fridge. Now get it sliced into wee squares (or big ones if you're a hallion) and get the kettle on.

Pineapple Delights

These are another Northern Irish classic and are duelling it out with the Fifteens (see page 113) for who takes the top spot in traybakes. These beauts roll back the years for me!

Baking brings people together in many ways and sometimes it can bring comfort. A while back, one of my best mates, Jelly, sadly lost his Granda. He got onto me as he wanted to have some traditional Northern Irish bakes for the family. I got to work. Pineapple Delights were one of his mum Karen's favourites, so they were non-negotiable. The family loved all the treats. I hope they brought some comfort during a tough time. Baking for others is truly special. You can make a lot of difference to someone's life with a small gesture like a wee box of buns.

MAKES ABOUT 12

For the base
225g digestive biscuits
110g salted butter

For the buttercream
110g unsalted butter, softened
175g icing sugar, sifted
1 tbsp double cream
½ tsp vanilla extract

For the topping
300ml double cream
1 x 435g tin of crushed pineapple, well drained
100g milk chocolate, grated (or a few crumbly Flake-style chocolate bars)

1 Preheat the oven to 140°C fan/160°C/gas 3. Line an 18 x 23cm (7 x 9in) baking tin with baking paper.

2 Blitz the digestive biscuits in a food processor or crush them up finely in a bowl.

3 Gently melt the butter for the base over a low heat, then pour this into your bowl of finely crushed biscuits. Mix it all together.

4 Line the base of your prepared baking tin with the mixture, press it down firmly and smoothing it out with the back of a spoon or a palette knife. Bake for 10–15 minutes just to firm and crisp it slightly. Remove from the oven and set aside to cool fully.

5 For the buttercream layer, beat your butter well until it's pale and fluffy. Then add the icing sugar and beat until smooth. Finally, add the cream and vanilla extract, giving it one last mix together. Spread this carefully over your cooled biscuit base, making sure you don't pull away the biscuit and wreck it.

6 For the topping, whip the cream and add the crushed pineapple. Gently fold this together, then spread the mixture evenly on top of the buttercream layer. You can ruffle the top with your palette knife or a fork to give it a nice finish.

7 Pop it into the fridge for about 4 hours to set, or overnight if you have the patience.

8 Grate some chocolate or break the crumbly chocolate bar over the top, then cut into slices.

Crispy Toffee Squares

These were always a firm favourite as a kid growing up. I'm not quite sure if Mum and Nanny made these for us because they were so simple or genuinely because they taste so good. Either way, a love for them is ingrained in my heart and tastebuds. They're a great wee bake for kids to get involved with and will hopefully kick off a lifetime of memories and fun in the kitchen.

MAKES ABOUT 12

140g salted butter
5 caramel nougat bars (such as Mars bars)
140g rice puff cereal (such as Rice Krispies)
200g milk chocolate, chopped

1 In a saucepan, gently melt the butter and caramel nougat bars over a low heat, gently stirring until fully combined.

2 Add the rice puff cereal and mix until each puff is coated and the mixture is fully combined. Tip into a 20cm (8in) square cake tin and smooth out the top.

3 Pop into the fridge for about 20–30 minutes to cool slightly.

4 Melt the chocolate over a bain-marie or in 30-second bursts in the microwave, then pour it over the crispy base, smoothing out the top. Pop it back into the fridge and allow to set firm.

5 Slice into squares and remove from the tin with a palette knife. Enjoy and feel like a big kid again or pass on a little nostalgia to the special young'ins in your life.

Tip

You can multiply these quantities if you want a thicker, more substantial bun, but unless you are using a larger tin there is no need to increase the chocolate or you'll need the hacksaw out to cut through it.

Flapjacks

These flapjacks are buttery, chewy and perfect for a quick breakfast or an afternoon snack. They are so simple to rustle up and are a great batch bake for the week ahead. I created this recipe when I started my wee wholesale bakery in Galway and they were a big hit. It's where things really kickstarted on this new journey and I'll always hold these recipes close. Not just because they're my favourites, but because they have so much significance in getting me where I am today.

MAKES ABOUT 12

385g porridge oats
150g mixed dried fruit
100g nuts of choice, chopped (optional)
175g salted butter, melted
125g soft light brown sugar
150g golden syrup

1. Preheat the oven to 160°C fan/180°C/gas 4. Line a 20 x 30cm (8 x 12in) deep baking tin with greaseproof paper.
2. Combine the porridge oats, dried fruit and chopped nuts (if using) in a large mixing bowl.
3. Melt the butter in a saucepan over a medium-low heat, then add the sugar and stir until dissolved. Add the golden syrup and stir until combined.
4. Pour the wet mixture into the dry ingredients and mix until fully combined. Tip into your prepared baking tin, pressing it down and smoothing it out with a spatula.
5. Bake for 20 minutes until slightly golden on top.
6. Remove from the oven and use the back of a spoon to carefully press and smooth out the top once more. Allow to cool fully before removing from the tin and slicing. Enjoy as a quick breakfast, afternoon snack or right away with your favourite cuppa!

Paradise Slice

This is a classic from my nanny's recipe collection and one of my favourites. Some might view this one as old fashioned, but the old ones are always the best. Packed with fruit and nuts, along with the flaky buttery pastry, this honestly is the perfect combination. The mixture is so delicate and soft, with added texture from the plump fruit and crunchy nuts, you will be refilling your cuppa for an excuse to have another slice.

MAKES ABOUT 12

- 1 x batch of Shortcrust Pastry (store-bought or see page 212)
- plain flour, for dusting
- 170g salted butter
- 170g caster sugar, plus extra for dusting
- 2 eggs
- 85g rice flour
- 85g ground almonds
- 1 tsp vanilla extract
- 85g glacé cherries, chopped
- 115g raisins
- 85g dried apricots, chopped
- 85g walnuts, chopped
- apricot jam, for spreading

1. Preheat the oven to 160°C fan/180°C/gas 4.
2. Roll out the shortcrust pastry on a lightly floured work surface to roughly the shape of your rectangular baking tin (mine is 18 x 25cm/7 x 10in and 2–3cm/1in deep). Roll the pastry onto your tin and press it gently into the edges. Trim off any excess pastry with a knife.
3. Add the butter and sugar to a mixing bowl and beat until pale and fluffy. Add the eggs and beat until combined, then add the rice flour and mix until combined. Do the same with the ground almonds. When the mixture is smooth, add the vanilla extract and beat well. Pop in your glacé cherries, raisins, apricots and walnuts, folding each time to ensure they are evenly distributed.
4. Spread a layer of apricot jam over your pastry before scooping your filling on top. Spread this out gently, so you don't mix it together with the jam and smooth out the top.
5. Bake for 30–35 minutes until nicely browned on top.
6. Allow to cool in the tin before slicing and carefully removing. These are very delicate when warm. Dust with caster sugar and there you have another classic bake ready to be devoured.

Loved by Alfie

A good lot of fruit in them!'

Apple and Berry Crumble Squares

These are a perfect autumn bake for using up Bramley apples, but they hit the spot all year round to be honest. They'll satisfy a craving for a traditional crumble, but in a smaller form – perfect with a cuppa or lathered in some warm custard. Chewy, buttery crumble with a sweet and tart fruit centre – what's not to love?

MAKES ABOUT 12

For the crumble
100g rolled oats
200g soft light brown sugar
250g plain flour
½ tsp mixed spice (optional)
125g salted butter, melted
1 egg
50g nuts of choice, chopped

For the filling
1–2 Bramley apples (about 150g)
200g frozen mixed berries (I generally use blackberries and raspberries)
1 tbsp soft light brown sugar
1 tbsp plain flour

1 Preheat the oven to 180°C fan/200°C/gas 6. Line a 20cm (8in) square baking tin with greaseproof paper.

2 Add the oats, light brown sugar, flour and mixed spice (if using) to a large mixing bowl and stir to combine.

3 Prepare your apples by peeling, coring and chopping into small cubes. Add these to a separate bowl along with the frozen berries, light brown sugar and flour. Mix together with a spoon until fully combined and your fruit is covered in the dry ingredients.

4 Pour the melted butter into the flour mixture along with the egg and combine with a spoon the best you can. You will eventually have to get your hands involved to finish the job. Run the mixture through your fingertips and it will form into a nice crumble consistency.

5 Add two-thirds of the crumble to the prepared baking tin and press it in roughly with your hands. Add the fruit filling on top of this and spread it out evenly with your hands. Add your chopped nuts to the remainder of your crumble and spread it over the top of the filling. Do this by crumbling it over with your hands to create an even layer over your fruit.

6 Bake for 35–40 minutes until golden on top.

7 Allow to cool fully in the tin before slicing as it will be delicate when warm. Alternatively, you can scoop it into a bowl straight away and enjoy with some fresh custard or vanilla ice cream.

Sweet Buns and Breads

Cinnamon Buns

It's hard to look past a fresh, pillowy cinnamon roll, especially when they have your kitchen smelling like a wee bakery. I created these ones for my old housemate Jack, because he goes absolutely daft for them. They are surprisingly simple to make, as they are a single-prove recipe, and are so delicious. You won't look past these for a weekend bake once you give them a go.

MAKES 10–12

350g plain flour, plus extra for dusting
½ tsp salt
50g caster sugar
3 tbsp (45g) butter
180ml whole milk
2½ tsp (7g packet) instant dried (fast-action) yeast
1 large egg, lightly beaten
vegetable oil, for greasing

For the filling
3 tbsp (45g) softened butter
70g soft light or dark brown sugar
1 tbsp ground cinnamon

For the cream cheese icing
115g full-fat cream cheese
2 tbsp (30g) softened butter
80g icing sugar
1 tsp vanilla extract

1 Add the flour, salt and caster sugar to a large mixing bowl and whisk together.

2 Melt the butter along with the milk to lukewarm, then add the yeast, whisking until it has dissolved.

3 Pour the milk mixture into your dry ingredients along with the egg and mix with a spoon until it forms a soft dough.

4 Turn the dough out onto a lightly floured work surface and knead for about 5 minutes. If it's very sticky, dust lightly with some flour. It will form a smooth dough ball. (You can also do this in a stand mixer fitted with a dough hook.)

5 Pop the dough into a lightly oiled bowl and cover loosely with a tea towel. Leave to rest for 10 minutes.

6 Meanwhile, combine all the filling ingredients in a bowl, mixing with a spoon until fully combined.

7 Use a rolling pin to roll out the dough to a rectangle, about 20 x 35cm. Spread the cinnamon mixture over the surface of the dough, then roll it up from the long edge into a tight log. Cut the log into 10–12 pieces and place them (spirals facing up) in a lightly oiled 23–25cm (9–10in) baking tin. Cover with some kitchen foil and leave to rest in a a warm place for about 1–1½ hours, or until doubled in size.

8 Meanwhile, preheat the oven to 170°C fan/190°C/gas 5.

9 Bake the rolls for 20–25 minutes, or until the internal temperature is 90°C on a probe thermometer. Remove from the oven and let them cool slightly in the tin.

10 For the icing, beat the cream cheese and butter in a bowl until smooth. Add the icing sugar and vanilla, and beat again until smooth. Spread this over the top of your cinnamon rolls. The glorious smell will make your kitchen a magnet for people and these are a sight to behold.

Almond Buns

I got this recipe from my Nanny Mamie's never-ending supply. They're a little like mini Bakewell tarts, only better! You have a lovely light, crumbly shortcrust pastry at the bottom, then a layer of raspberry jam (I'm hoping you're reaching for your homemade Raspberry Jam – page 215), topped off with a chewy almond meringue. It has all the textures you want with a heap of flavour too, so get your apron on and get baking.

MAKES 24

1 x batch of Shortcrust Pastry (store-bought or see page 212)
plain flour, for dusting
Raspberry Jam (store-bought or see page 215)
flaked almonds, to decorate
caster sugar, for sprinkling

For the almond filling
225g caster sugar
115g ground almonds
2 tbsp farola flour or semolina
2 eggs
a few drops of almond extract
1 tsp water

1. Preheat the oven to 150°C fan/170°C/gas 3.
2. Roll out the pastry on a lightly floured work surface to about 3–5mm thick. Cut out 24 pastry rounds using a floured pastry cutter or glass that is similar in size to your cupcake/bun tins. Place the pastry rounds into the tins.
3. Dollop ½ teaspoon of raspberry jam into each pastry case.
4. For the almond filling, add the sugar, ground almonds and farola/semolina to a mixing bowl. Mix until well combined. In a separate bowl, whisk the eggs, then add the almond extract to the eggs and whisk again. Pour this into your dry ingredients and mix well. Finally, add the water and give it one last mix, making sure everything is fully incorporated.
5. Top each pastry case with a teaspoon of the almond filling mixture. Sprinkle a few flaked almonds on top and add another sprinkling of caster sugar.
6. Bake for about 15–20 minutes, or until golden brown and fully cooked on top. Leave them to sit in the tin for a few minutes before removing to a wire cooling rack. Leave to cool for a further 10 minutes. The handiest way to get them out of the tin is to pry them out with a wee knife before tucking in.

Loved by Alfie

'Nice meringue-like top on these.'

Raspberry and Frangipane Buns

These may seem fancy and difficult, but they're so simple to rustle up. I've always had these as slices, but you could also serve it up as a delicious tart with a dollop of fresh cream. The pairing of raspberry and almond has always been a classic. These slices are perfect for a summer dessert or afternoon tea, and you will be surprised how light and delicate they are. Once you try them, you will be looking for an excuse to make them every week.

MAKES ABOUT 12

1 x batch of Shortcrust Pastry (store-bought or see page 212)
plain flour, for dusting
175g butter, softened
200g caster sugar, plus extra for sprinkling
4 medium eggs
75g self-raising flour
200g ground almonds
a few drops of almond extract
2 tbsp milk
4 tbsp Raspberry Jam (store-bought or see page 215)
300g raspberries

1. Preheat the oven to 170°C fan/190°C/gas 5.
2. Roll out your pastry on a lightly floured work surface to a rectangle, 25 x 35cm and 5mm thick. Roll the pastry onto a 23 x 33cm (9 x 13in) lipped baking tray, tucking the pastry up the sides of the tray. Trim any excess pastry off with a knife and prick the base of the pastry all over with a fork. Place a sheet of greaseproof paper on top and fill with baking beans.
3. Bake for 15 minutes, then remove the greaseproof paper and baking beans. Reduce the oven temperature to 160°C fan/180°C/gas 4 and bake for a further 10 minutes until the pastry is a pale golden colour. Remove from the oven and leave to cool.
4. For the frangipane filling, cream together the butter and sugar until pale and fluffy. Gradually add the eggs and flour, mixing continuously. Do the same with the ground almonds until they're fully combined. Finally, add the almond extract and milk, mixing one last time.
5. Once the pastry case has cooled, spread an even layer of raspberry jam over the base. Spoon your frangipane filling over the jam and gently smooth it out. Place the fresh raspberries on top, gently pressing them into the filling slightly.
6. Pop it into the oven at 160°C fan/180°C/gas 4 for 30–35 minutes until golden on top and springy to the touch.
7. Sprinkle the top with some caster sugar and leave to cool in the tin. Once cooled, slice it up and get stuck in!

Loved by Alfie

'Lovely and tangy but light.'

Meringue Coconut Buns

If you're a fan of coconut, you will love these wee bundles of joy. I got this recipe from my nanny – she always rustled these up for me when I was younger. They have a lovely chew from the meringue topping. Paired with some homemade raspberry jam and buttery shortcrust pastry, there aren't many bite-size treats that go down quite as well as these.

MAKES 24

- 1 x batch of Shortcrust Pastry (store-bought or see page 212)
- plain flour, for dusting
- 100g Raspberry Jam (store-bought or see page 215)
- 4 egg whites
- 225g caster sugar
- 170g desiccated coconut

1. Preheat the oven to 160°C fan/180°C/gas 4.
2. Roll out the shortcrust pastry out on a lightly floured work surface to about 5mm thick. Cut out 24 pastry rounds using a floured pastry cutter or glass that is similar in size to your cupcake/bun tins. Place the pastry rounds into the tins.
3. Dollop about ½ teaspoon of raspberry jam into each pastry case.
4. In a large bowl, lightly whisk the egg whites for a few minutes to break them up, then continue to whisk on a high speed while gradually adding the sugar. Whisk until you have a shiny and smooth meringue. Add the desiccated coconut and fold through.
5. Pop about a tablespoon of meringue into each pastry case, ensuring they are full and that the raspberry jam is covered. Make sure you don't over-fill them.
6. Bake for 20–25 minutes, or until the meringue is nicely golden on top.
7. Allow to cool in the tin for about 10 minutes, then prise out with a knife and place on a wire cooling rack. Leave to cool fully. These are chewy, bite-size bundles of joy and you will go mad for them.

Mum's Cornflake Cream Buns

These are a simple, yet delicious, wee bun that my mum would rustle up, and they are a perfect thing to make at short notice that will still impress. They are chocolatey, buttery and have a lovely crunch from the cornflakes. Not complicated at all, so this is a brilliant recipe to get the kids involved with. Even if it's just to lick the spoons clean, which I still do on occasion!

MAKES ABOUT 12

- 115g butter
- 3 tbsp golden syrup
- 200g milk chocolate, chopped
- 200g cornflakes
- 250ml whipping cream
- 2 tbsp icing sugar
- 50g flaky chocolate (like a Cadbury's Flake bar), to decorate

1. Combine the butter, golden syrup and chocolate in a saucepan and melt over a low–medium heat, stirring occasionally.
2. Add the cornflakes to the melted mixture. Stir until fully combined.
3. Line a 23cm (9in) square baking tin with greaseproof paper, leaving a slight overhang to make the traybake easier to remove.
4. Pop the cornflake mixture into the prepared tin and gently level it out and press it down. Refrigerate for about 1 hour until set.
5. Whip together the cream and icing sugar, then spread it all over the chilled cornflake base. Crumble the flaky chocolate over the top.
6. Remove from the tin and slice up into your desired size. This is hands-down one of the easiest recipes, but it still packs a punch on flavour.

Butterfly Buns

These wee buns were another of Mum's specials and now they are something I love to make too. A light and fluffy sponge topped with sweet, thick cream makes for the perfect combination. We like to use mock cream to fill these, but buttercream or fresh cream is perfect as well. It's an all-in-one method, so they are quick and easy to rustle up. Plus, they look great.

MAKES ABOUT 18

For the cupcakes
225g soft margarine
225g caster sugar
225g self-raising flour, sifted
4 eggs, lightly beaten
piping jelly (gel) in your favourite colour, or a few spoonfuls of your favourite jam
icing sugar, for dusting

For the mock cream
80ml water
115g caster sugar
225g unsalted butter, softened
1 tsp vanilla extract
60g icing sugar, sifted

1 Preheat the oven to 170°C fan/190°C/gas 5. Line your cupcake/bun tins with paper cases and set aside.

2 Add all of the cupcake ingredients to a large mixing bowl or stand mixer and beat together until light and fluffy. You will have to scrape the bottom and sides of the bowl from time to time, to ensure everything is well combined.

3 Spoon the mixture evenly into your bun cases and bake for 15–20 minutes until the tops are lightly golden and an inserted skewer comes out clean.

4 Allow to cool in the tin for a few minutes, then transfer to a wire cooling rack and leave to cool fully.

5 For the mock cream, combine the water and caster sugar in a pan set over a low–medium heat. Stir regularly to dissolve the sugar. Bring to the boil, then reduce to a simmer for 5 minutes. Remove from the heat and leave to cool completely. (You can prepare this earlier or the night before to save time. You can also pop it into the fridge or a cold water bath to speed up the cooling process.)

6 Cream the butter in a stand mixer or in a large mixing bowl until pale. Add the vanilla and mix until well combined. While continuously whisking, slowly pour in the cold sugar syrup until it is fully combined. Gradually add the icing sugar in the same way, continuously mixing on a low speed until it is combined. Finally, beat on a high speed for a few minutes, or until the mixture becomes pale and creamy.

7 Once the buns have cooled, cut a small upside-down cone shape out of the top of each bun and cut in half to make 'wings'. Pop the mock cream into a piping bag fitted with a star nozzle and pipe a swirl of cream on top of each bun. Place each 'wing' on either side of the cream to resemble butterfly wings. Add a small blob of piping jelly or jam to the centre of each cake for the butterfly 'body'. Dust with icing sugar and then dig in. Try not to eat too many – they are addictive!

Cheesecake Buns

These aren't what you first think of when you hear the word 'cheesecake', but I was raised to know these by that name and I think many others were too, with slight variations, such as 'Welsh cheesecake'. With a buttery shortcrust pastry base, these are filled with jam and a light sponge topping, then drizzled with icing – it's a match made in heaven. I challenge you not to have more than one with a cuppa, because if I'm honest I could probably do double figures.

MAKES 24

1 x batch of Shortcrust Pastry (store-bought or see page 212)
plain flour, for dusting
Raspberry Jam (store-bought or see page 215)
170g salted butter, softened
170g caster sugar
170g self-raising flour
30g ground almonds
3 eggs, lightly beaten
1 tsp vanilla extract

To decorate
150g icing sugar mixed with enough water to make a thick, drizzling icing
50g flaked almonds

Loved by Alfie

'They just hit the spot with a cuppa tae.'

1. Preheat the oven to 160°C fan/180°C/gas 4.
2. Roll out the pastry on a lightly floured work surface to about 5mm thick. Cut out 24 discs with a floured 6cm pastry cutter and place each disc into your bun tins.
3. Place ½ teaspoon of raspberry jam into each pastry case.
4. Beat the butter and sugar in a mixing bowl until smooth and fluffy.
5. Add the self-raising flour and ground almonds to a separate bowl and combine with a spoon.
6. Gradually add the eggs and flour mixture to the butter mixture, alternating between each and mixing between each addition. Finally, add the vanilla and beat this through.
7. Place 1 tablespoon of the batter into each pastry case, covering the jam.
8. Bake for about 30 minutes, or until nicely browned on top. Allow them to cool in the tin for about 5–10 minutes before transferring to a wire cooling rack.
9. Once they are fully cooled, drizzle some of your icing on top and sprinkle over a few flaked almonds. These wee buns are mouthfuls of joy and you will love them.

Jonny's Wee Raspberry Tarts

My little sister and me were honestly addicted to these, back in the day. I used to buy a packet of four on my school lunch break on a Friday and polish the lot off. That might sound outrageous, but if you've had them, you'll understand. They're so moreish with the buttery shortcrust pastry, sweet raspberry jam, cream and icing. Surprisingly simple to make, even though others might think you're pulling out all the stops when you produce them.

MAKES 12

butter, for greasing
½ x batch of Rich Shortcrust Pastry (store-bought or see page 212)
plain flour, for dusting
Raspberry Jam (store-bought or see page 215)

For the cream filling
300ml double cream
3 tbsp icing sugar

For the icing
300g icing sugar
3–4 tbsp water
pink food colouring

1 Preheat the oven to 160°C fan/180°C/gas 4. Lightly grease a 12-hole bun tray.

2 Roll out your pastry on a lightly floured work surface to about 5mm thick. Cut out 12 pastry shells out with a floured 6cm pastry cutter or a round cutter slightly bigger than the cups of your bun tray. Pop each pastry shell into the prepared tray, gently pressing each one in to ensure no air is trapped at the bottom or sides.

3 With a fork, prick a few holes into the base of each pastry shell, before lining them with some greaseproof paper or a paper cupcake case. Fill with some baking beans and bake for 15 minutes. Remove the paper or cupcake cases and baking beans, then bake for a further 5 minutes until golden. Allow to rest in the tin for a few minutes before removing to a wire cooling rack to cool fully.

4 Once cooled, spoon 1 teaspoon of jam into each pastry shell.

5 For the cream filling, whip together the cream and icing sugar in a bowl. Transfer to a piping bag and pipe a little cream, about the size of a ping-pong ball, on top of each jam-filled pastry shell (spoon on your cream if you don't have a piping bag to hand). Leave a slight gap between your pastry and cream, just enough to allow any overflow of icing to pool like a small moat. Place into the fridge for about 15 minutes while you make the icing.

6 Add the icing sugar to a bowl and gradually add the water, stirring until you get a just-pourable consistency. Add the pink food colouring until you get your desired colour – a bright pink is perfect.

7 Top each pastry shell with a teaspoon of icing. Once it has run down the cream, you can see where you might have to add a little more. Allow the icing to set before getting stuck in.

Chocolate Éclairs

There has been many an argument in our house when someone has eaten Dad's chocolate éclairs from the fridge. The older I get, I understand his frustration. Knowing something's at home in the fridge waiting for you, only to be welcomed with an empty plate in the sink – terrible! These are so light with the choux pastry piped full of cream and the delicious thick chocolate glaze. I've found that the best way to avoid arguments is just to make up a new batch.

MAKES 6–8

1 x batch of Choux Pastry (see page 214)
vegetable oil, for greasing
250ml double cream, whipped

For the chocolate glaze
175g chocolate (50–60% cocoa solids), well broken up (or use chocolate chips)
100ml double cream
pinch of salt
15g unsalted butter, cubed and softened

1 Make your choux pastry according to the instructions on page 214 and spoon into a piping bag.

2 Meanwhile, preheat the oven to 200°C fan/220°C/gas 7 and lightly grease two large baking sheets.

3 Pipe 7–8cm sausage shapes of pastry onto your prepared baking sheets, spacing them well apart to allow room for expansion.

4 Bake for about 20–25 minutes until risen, golden and crisp.

5 Remove from the oven and cut a slit along one side of each bun with a sharp knife – this allows the steam to escape. Pop them back into the oven for another 2 minutes to crisp a little more, then place them on a wire cooling rack to cool fully.

6 For the chocolate glaze, add your chocolate to a large bowl. Place the cream and salt in a saucepan and gently heat over a medium–high heat, whisking regularly so it doesn't stick or burn on the bottom of the pan. Just as the cream starts to simmer and prior to boiling, remove from the heat and immediately pour over your chocolate. Add the butter and mix until the chocolate has completely melted and you have a glossy glaze.

7 Pipe each cooled éclair with a healthy amount of the whipped cream, then dip the tops in the chocolate glaze, allowing any excess to drip back off into the bowl. Alternatively, you can pipe the chocolate glaze on top. Pop these back onto your wire cooling rack and allow the glaze to set. Eat immediately, if you don't mind a bit of runny chocolate – or pop in the fridge and chill before enjoying.

Cinnamon Pecan Plait

This is a twist on my chocolate babka recipe. It stemmed from my nanny's love of pecans. Ever since I tried her Pecan Pie (see page 170), I wanted to rustle up something that she would love. This one definitely pairs well with a strong cup of coffee. If you love your dried fruit, the option is there to add some.

MAKES 1 LOAF

For the dough
275g plain flour, plus extra for dusting
5g instant dried (fast-action) yeast
25g caster sugar
½ tsp salt
2 eggs, lightly beaten
50ml whole milk
80g butter, cubed and softened

For the filling
100g butter, softened
80g light brown sugar
1 tbsp ground cinnamon
80g pecans, finely chopped
80g raisins (optional)

For the sugar syrup
100g caster sugar
100ml water

1 To start the filling, add the softened butter to a bowl along with the light brown sugar and ground cinnamon. Mix with a spoon until combined and smooth. Set aside.

2 For the dough, sift the flour into a bowl, adding the yeast to one side. Add the caster sugar and salt to the opposite side, then create a well in the middle using a spoon. Add the eggs and milk to the well and mix it all together with a spoon until roughly combined. Add the softened butter and mix well. It will start to form a wet, sticky dough.

3 Turn the dough out onto a lightly floured surface and dust the top with some flour. Begin kneading. It will be quite sticky, so add a little flour if needed, but don't get carried away as it will start to come together as you knead. Knead for about 10 minutes until it becomes smooth and silky. Alternatively, use a stand mixer fitted with a dough hook.

4 Roll the dough out on a lightly floured surface to a 40 x 30cm rectangle. Spread the cinnamon filling mixture over this, then sprinkle over the chopped pecans and raisins (if using). Roll it up tightly from the longest edge, keeping the seam hidden underneath and neatly tuck each end in.

5 With a knife or pizza cutter, slice it down the middle lengthways, to give you two separate pieces of dough. With the cut edges facing up, seal both ends together by firmly squeezing them. Plait your two pieces of dough, lapping one over the other and seal the ends firmly together. Pop this into a lined 900g (2lb) loaf tin and cover with a clean tea towel. Leave to rise for 2 hours, or until it doubles in size.

6 Meanwhile, preheat the oven to 170°C fan/190°C/gas 5

7 Bake the loaf for 15 minutes, then reduce the oven temperature to 150°C fan/170°C/gas 4 and bake for another 25–30 minutes until golden on top and an inserted skewer comes out clean.

8 While it is baking, make your sugar syrup. Stir the sugar and water together in a saucepan until the sugar dissolves. Bring to the boil over a medium heat, then reduce to a simmer. Don't stir for about 5 minutes until it becomes syrupy.

9 Brush the hot loaf with the sugar syrup and leave it to cool in the tin for about 10 minutes before transferring to a wire cooling rack. This really does taste best slightly warm with a cup of coffee, but it is very delicate, so be gentle when you slice it up.

Iced Fruit Bannock

You might never have seen this sweet bread, or may have had a slightly different childhood equivalent. I loved it when this was produced at the lunch table on a Saturday after I returned home from mini rugby. Slathered in real butter and homemade jam, it's soft and sweet, almost like a brioche, only it has more of a chew and is packed with pieces of juicy fruit. This is a delight and will always bring me back to my youth.

SERVES 4

120ml whole milk, plus (optional) extra for brushing
40g caster sugar
10g instant dried (fast-action) yeast
400g strong bread flour, plus extra for dusting
1½ tsp salt
40g salted butter
120ml lukewarm water
vegetable oil, for greasing
150g sultanas
100g glacé cherries
1 tsp ground cinnamon

For the icing

200g icing sugar mixed with enough water to give a thick, spreadable icing
75g desiccated coconut

1 Slightly warm the milk, then add the caster sugar and yeast. Leave for a few minutes until it activates and the surface is foaming.

2 Sift the strong bread flour into a large mixing bowl along with the salt. Add the butter and rub this in until combined and the mixture resembles breadcrumbs. Add the milky yeast mixture along with the water and stir until combined.

3 Turn the mixture out onto a lightly floured work surface and dust with a small amount of flour. Knead for around 5 minutes until smooth and it bounces back when lightly pressed with a finger.

4 Place in a lightly oiled bowl and cover with a clean tea towel or cling film. Leave to rise in a slightly warm spot for about 1 hour until it doubles in size.

5 Place the dough on a clean work surface and push out flat using your fingers. Add most of the sultanas and glacé cherries, and sprinkle over the ground cinnamon. Fold the dough over and knead until incorporated, then add the rest of the fruit, kneading once again until evenly distributed.

6 You can either shape it into a loaf (as shown on page 55) and place on a baking tray, or place in a greased 20–23cm (8–9in) cake tin. Cover and leave to prove for another hour until doubled in size.

7 Meanwhile, preheat the oven to 180°C fan/200°C/gas 6.

8 Brush the top with some milk if you prefer a deeper browned top. Bake for 45 minutes until risen with a rich brown colour on top. If you feel it is browning too much, you can cover with some kitchen foil during the bake. The bread will be ready when you tap the bottom and it sounds hollow. Allow to rest for 5 minutes before placing on a wire cooling rack. This is delicious when slightly warm with some real butter, but I feel that the texture is much better and it's tastier when cooled.

9 Cover the top of your loaf with your icing and sprinkle with desiccated coconut. Leave to set before slicing.

Loved by Alfie

'Plastered in butter and jam – hard to beat!'

Fruited Soda Farls

These are a staple Northern Irish recipe, similar to a soda bannock, but quite separate. Back in the day, these would have been rustled up daily in kitchens all over the country. My Granda Alfie has fond memories of his nanny making them, to be eaten fresh off the griddle with butter dripping down your hand. You will be blown away by how soft and tasty these are. I really hope you enjoy them as much as me.

MAKES 4

340g soda bread flour, plus extra for dusting
140g sultanas or plump raisins
285ml buttermilk
1 tbsp sunflower oil (or any vegetable oil)

1. Sift the flour into a mixing bowl and add your chosen dried fruit, mixing with your hand to combine.
2. Combine the buttermilk and oil in a jug, mixing with a spoon. Gradually add this to the bowl, mixing with a fork between each addition until it all comes together with no dry patches of flour left.
3. Turn the mixture out onto a lightly floured work surface and dust the top with a little more flour. Gently knead to form a soft ball of dough. Shape it into a circle, then roll it out to about 1cm thick. Use a floured knife to cut it into quarters and dust the tops with more flour.
4. Heat a griddle or dry frying pan over a medium–high heat. When hot, add the farls, floured side down, and cook for 2 minutes to start developing the crust. Now turn the heat down to medium and cook for a further 8–10 minutes until it has formed a nice crust.
5. Dust the tops of the farls with some more flour before flipping and repeating the same cooking process. Once you have both sides baked with a lovely crust, stand them up on their sides and cook for a few minutes, turning as needed, just to seal and bake off the edges.
6. Wrap in a light tea towel or muslin cloth and place on a wire cooling rack. This will lock in the heat and moisture, softening them and leaving you with beautiful sodas. Now slice them up, plaster in real butter and top with whatever you feel like adding.

Treacle Soda Farls

This takes the traditional soda farl to another level. I definitely haven't seen these outside of home in Northern Ireland. The treacle gives a lovely deep flavour and makes the crust and consistency that bit more chewy. My nanny adores treacle, so this recipe was always going to be included. I think her love for it, just like baking, has firmly rubbed off on me too.

MAKES 4

340g plain flour, plus extra for dusting
40g caster sugar
1 tsp salt
1 tsp bicarbonate of soda
small knob of salted butter
handful of sultanas (optional)
1 tbsp double cream
2 tbsp treacle
up to 285ml buttermilk, as needed

1 Sift the flour, sugar, salt and bicarb into a mixing bowl. Mix together with your hands and then work the butter through the mix using your fingertips to rub it in. You can add some sultanas at this point and combine, but it's totally down to preference.

2 In a small bowl, mix together the cream and treacle. Add a little of the treacle mixture to the mixing bowl along with a little of the buttermilk and combine with a fork. Repeat this process until you have used all the treacle mixture, mixing until you get a soft dough and there are no dry spots left. You may not need all the buttermilk – you don't want the mixture to be too wet, so be sure to add it gradually.

3 Pop the mixture onto a lightly floured work surface and lightly dust the top with some flour. Gently knead until it forms a soft ball of dough. Shape it into a circle, then roll it out to about 1cm thick. Use a floured knife to cut it into quarters and dust the tops with more flour.

4 Heat a griddle or dry frying pan over a medium–high heat. When hot, add the farls, floured side down, and cook for 2–3 minutes to start developing the crust. Now turn the heat down to medium and cook for a further 8–10 minutes until it has formed a nice crust.

5 Dust the tops of the farls with some more flour before flipping and repeating the same cooking process. Once you have both sides baked with a lovely crust, stand them up on their sides and cook for a few minutes, turning as needed, just to seal and bake off the edges.

6 Wrap in a light tea towel or muslin cloth and place on a wire cooling rack. This will lock in the heat and moisture, softening them and leaving you with beautiful sodas. You can eat them immediately, but they are very delicate when warm and the cloth will help soften the crusts. Eat slightly warm with some real butter and maybe a few wedges of cheese.

Loved by Alfie

'Real butter and cheese on this is something else.'

Monkey Bread

Monkey bread is one of the best tear-and-share breads out there. Served warm, fresh out of the oven, it's delicious. It's perfect for a weekend brunch or a special treat or dessert for any holiday or occasion. You will be licking your fingers clean from the tasty sticky glaze and there might be a few fall outs if someone gets more than their fair share.

SERVES 6–8

240ml whole milk, slightly warmed
80ml lukewarm water
50g caster sugar
2 tbsp unsalted butter, melted
2¼ tsp instant dried (fast-action) yeast
500g plain flour, plus extra for dusting
2 tsp salt
vegetable oil or cooking spray, for greasing

For the brown sugar coating
200g soft light brown sugar
2 tsp ground cinnamon
115g unsalted butter, melted

For the glaze
115g icing sugar
2 tbsp whole milk
50–75g pecans (or nuts of choice), chopped

1 Add the milk, water, sugar, melted butter and yeast to a measuring jug and mix until combined.

2 Add the flour and salt to a large mixing bowl or a stand mixer fitted with a dough hook and begin mixing on a low speed. Gradually add your milk mixture. Once a dough comes together, increase the speed to medium and mix for about 6–7 minutes until the dough is smooth and shiny. Turn the dough out onto a lightly floured work surface and knead briefly to form a smooth, round ball. (If you're kneading by hand, whisk together your flour and salt in a large mixing bowl. Make a well in the centre and pour in the milk mixture. Stir together with a wooden spoon until a shaggy dough forms, then transfer to a lightly floured surface and knead until the dough is soft and shiny.)

3 Lightly oil or spray a large bowl and place the dough in this, turning to coat the surface of the dough lightly in oil. Cover the bowl with a clean tea towel or some cling film and place in a warm spot for 1 hour, or until the dough has doubled in size.

4 For the brown sugar coating, add the brown sugar and cinnamon to a bowl. Melt the butter in a separate bowl and set both aside.

5 Gently remove the dough from the bowl and place it on a clean surface. Pat it into a 20cm square, then use a knife or pizza slicer to cut into roughly 60 pieces. Take each piece of dough and roll into a ball.

6 One at a time, dip each dough ball into the melted butter, allowing any excess to drip back off into the bowl, then roll it in the brown sugar mix. Layer the coated balls in a greased 26cm (10in) bundt tin, staggering the seams where the dough balls meet. Repeat until all the dough is used up. Cover the tin tightly with some cling film and place in a warm spot for about 1 hour until the dough balls have puffed up and risen to about 3–5cm from the top of the tin.

7 Meanwhile, preheat the oven to 160°C fan/180°C/gas 4.

8 Remove the cling film and bake for 30–35 minutes until the top is a deep golden brown and caramel has begun to bubble around the edges. Allow to cool in the tin for 5 minutes, then turn out onto a serving plate and allow to cool for a further 10 minutes.

9 For the glaze, combine the icing sugar and milk in a small bowl, mixing until smooth. Use a whisk or spoon to drizzle this over your monkey bread, letting it run over the top and down the sides. Sprinkle over your chopped nuts. Serve when still slightly warm. This is absolutely delicious and you will be fighting to tear your fair share when it's served up!

Puddings

Rhubarb Tart

There's always a tart on the go when it comes to pudding time out our way. It's a toss up in our house for which is the best. It really comes down to rhubarb or apple, and since we have rhubarb growing in our vegetable garden, I had to include it. Then again, the filling is interchangeable in this recipe. I've seen my dad have this the next morning for breakfast many a time and I don't blame him. I'd do the same, but I know I'd be in the bad books if I ate it before him.

SERVES 8

- 1 x batch of Shortcrust Pastry (store-bought or see page 212)
- cornflour, for dusting
- 1 bunch of rhubarb, washed and chopped into chunks
- 8 heaped tbsp caster sugar, plus extra for sprinkling
- 1 egg, beaten

1. Preheat the oven to 160°C fan/180°C/gas 4.
2. Divide your pastry in half. Roll one half out on a floured surface to the size of a large dinner plate. You want it to be about 5mm thick. Use it to line a 23cm (9in) tart tin (or use an ovenproof dinner plate, like I do) and dust with a little cornflour. This helps to absorb any extra juices and thickens up the filling nicely.
3. Put a good layer of rhubarb over the base of your tart (roughly half of your rhubarb). Sprinkle a healthy amount of sugar over this – about 4 heaped tablespoons. Now repeat this process with the rest of your rhubarb and sprinkle with more sugar.
4. Wet the edges of your pastry (this will help it to stick) and trim off any excess pastry with a knife. Roll out the other half of the pastry and place this on top. Gently press down around the edges of your tart and trim off the excess pastry. Press down all around with the back of a fork to seal the edges. You can also use the back of a teaspoon or your thumb.
5. Egg wash the top of your tart, cut a small cross in the middle and prick all over the top with a fork. This allows some of the steam to be released when baking.
6. Bake for about 40 minutes, or until nicely golden on top. Sprinkle the top with some more caster sugar and serve it up with some fresh cream, custard or ice cream – the choice is yours. I can tell ye, if all three are available, I'm having the lot.

Loved by Alfie

'Lovely when warm with vanilla ice cream.'

Toffee Apple Crumble

This one is a change up on the old faithful apple crumble. Once you try it, you might never look back. It's almost like a self-saucing pudding. Served warm with some vanilla ice cream, it is right up there with the best. It turned a few heads in the house when I explained what I was trying to make, but when my Granda Alfie gave it the seal of approval, saying, 'A could eat it all no problem,' I knew I was on to a winner.

SERVES 6

5 Bramley apples, peeled, cored and chopped into chunks
butter, for greasing
50–100g dates, halved (optional)

For the toffee sauce
140g butter
140g soft dark brown sugar
225ml double cream

For the crumble topping
250g plain flour
1 tsp ground cinnamon
200g butter, cold and cubed
100g rolled oats
100g soft dark brown sugar
50–100g pecans, chopped (optional)

1 Preheat the oven to 180°C fan/200°C/gas 6.

2 To make the toffee sauce, add the butter, sugar and double cream to a large saucepan. Melt these down over a medium heat for about 10 minutes, gently simmering to thicken. Pour into a separate bowl and set aside.

3 Add the chopped apples to the same saucepan along with a few tablespoons of the toffee sauce. Gently stew these down for about 5–10 minutes until the apples have slightly softened.

4 For the crumble topping, add the flour and cinnamon to a bowl along with the butter. Gently work in the butter using your fingertips. It will start to resemble breadcrumbs. Now add the oats along with the soft dark brown sugar, continuing to work this through with your fingertips. Finally, mix in the chopped pecans (if using).

5 Tip the apples into a large greased baking dish and scatter over your dates (if using). Pour most of your toffee sauce over this, holding back enough to drizzle over the top when you serve it up.

6 Crumble over your topping (I'm sure this will spark a debate, but I love a 50/50 ratio when it comes to the crumble and filling).

7 Bake for about 30 minutes until the top is nicely golden and it's bubbling around the edges. You can allow it to cool slightly, but serving it up warm with vanilla ice cream, cream or custard is hard to beat.

Bakewell Tart

This will always be a classic in our house. When I was younger, I convinced myself these were only for 'big people', but ohhh boy was I wrong. That unmistakable flavour of almonds is such a great accompaniment to a cuppa – and we all love a cuppa.

SERVES 8

For the shortcrust pastry
225g plain flour, plus extra for dusting
150g unsalted butter, chilled and cubed
25g icing sugar
1 large egg, beaten

For the filling
85g unsalted butter, softened
85g caster sugar
½ tsp almond extract
3 eggs, beaten
55g ground almonds
55g self-raising flour
3–4 tbsp Raspberry Jam (store-bought or see page 215)

For the topping
300g icing sugar
½ tsp almond extract
small amount of cold water, as needed
pink food colouring

1 Preheat the oven to 160°C fan/180°C/gas 4.

2 Make the shortcrust pastry by adding the flour and butter to a food processor. Blitz until they resemble breadcrumbs. You can also do this in a bowl and use your fingertips to work the butter into the flour. Add the icing sugar and blitz, then gradually add the beaten egg while blitzing. It will come together and form a nice dough.

3 Turn the dough onto a lightly floured work surface and knead lightly to bring it together into a ball. Roll it out into a circle about 5mm thick and pop it into a 23cm (9in) fluted tart tin. Use a little bit of the excess pastry to push the pastry into the edges of your tin (this will help you avoid ripping the main pastry shell). Cover with some greaseproof paper and fill with baking beans.

4 Bake for 15 minutes, then remove the paper and baking beans. Trim any excess pastry and bake for another 10 minutes before removing and allowing to cool fully.

5 For the filling, beat the butter in a large bowl until pale and fluffy. Add the caster sugar and beat until it's fully combined. Add the almond extract along with the eggs and beat to combine Finally, add the ground almonds and self-raising flour, and combine well.

6 Spread a layer of raspberry jam on top of the cooled pastry shell and gently spoon the filling mixture on top of this. Carefully smooth it out and pop it into the oven at 160°C fan/180°C/gas 4 for about 35–40 minutes until the frangipane filling is firm and golden. Allow to cool fully before removing from the tin.

7 For the topping, mix the icing sugar and almond extract with a small amount of water until you get the desired spreadable consistency. Spread enough over the tart to cover, but hold a little back. Mix this with a few drops of pink food colouring until your get your desired colour. Pop the pink icing into a piping bag and drizzle lines across the top of the tart. Drag a toothpick or skewer across the pink stripes to create a feathered effect. Allow the icing to firm up slightly before slicing.

Sticky Toffee Pudding

I don't think anyone can argue that this isn't a truly classic pudding. I'm not sure I've ever seen a single dessert menu without one. This has a soft and moist sponge, full of that sweet date flavour as well as distinct, deep black treacle. The toffee sauce soaks through and it's hard to beat this served warm with some vanilla ice cream.

SERVES 6

80g salted butter, softened, plus extra for greasing
200g pitted dates, chopped
1 tsp bicarbonate of soda
200ml boiling water
150g plain flour
2 tsp baking powder
½ tsp sea salt (or ordinary salt)
60g soft dark brown sugar
2 eggs, lightly beaten
1 heaped tbsp black treacle

For the toffee sauce
150g salted butter
300g soft dark brown sugar
2 tbsp black treacle
200ml double cream

1 Preheat the oven to 160°C fan/180°C/gas 4 and grease a 23cm (9in) square baking dish.

2 Add the dates to a bowl along with the bicarbonate of soda and pour over the boiling water. Give this a stir and leave for about 10 minutes.

3 Add the flour, baking powder and salt to a bowl and whisk to combine. Set aside.

4 In a large mixing bowl, cream the dark brown sugar and butter together until pale and smooth. You will have to scrape down the sides of your bowl throughout the mixing process. Add the eggs and beat until combined, then add the black treacle (dipping your tablespoon in some boiling water first makes this easier). Beat until fully combined.

5 Sift the bowl of dry ingredients into the wet mixture and beat until incorporated and smooth.

6 Give your dates another stir with a fork, slightly squishing them, then add the entire mixture to the batter and fold through.

7 Pour the mixture into your greased dish and bake for about 30–35 minutes, or until an inserted skewer comes out clean.

8 While that's in the oven, make the toffee sauce. Add the butter, sugar and treacle to a saucepan and gently melt over a low heat, stirring until everything is combined. Add the cream and increase the heat to medium-high. When the mixture starts to bubble, remove from the heat and set aside.

9 Remove the sponge from the oven, prick it all over with a skewer and pour about a quarter of the warm toffee sauce over the top. Ease this to the edges with a spoon or spatula, ensuring that the sponge is completely covered with the thick sticky glaze. Let sit for about 20–30 minutes until it's a nice warm temperature.

10 Quickly reheat your sauce and serve big old scoops of pudding with lashings of sauce and either freshly whipped cream or ice cream.

Lemon Meringue Pie

My mum rustles these up all the time, especially in the sunnier months. I think it's a dessert you grow into – a bit like drinking wine. Once your gub gets a bit more cultured, things change. I can thank two of my best mates, Kyle and Carey, for that. They pulled me out of the country and showed me the wonders of the big city and the rest of the world. Now, the tart, fresh, lemon centre is my favourite bit of this pie and rather than a bottle of Buckfast wine I'm drinking Cab Sauv and Pinot Noir!

SERVES 8

For the pastry
175g plain flour, plus extra for dusting
15g icing sugar
75g butter, cubed
1 egg yolk
1 tbsp cold water

For the filling
zest and juice of 2 large lemons
40g cornflour
225ml water
75g caster sugar
2 egg yolks

For the meringue
3 egg whites
120g caster sugar

1 Preheat the oven to 180°C fan/200°C/gas 6.

2 Add the plain flour and icing sugar to a food processor and blitz, then add the butter and blitz until it starts to resemble breadcrumbs. You can also do this in a bowl using your fingertips. Add the egg yolk and water and blitz again until fully combined. Transfer to a bowl and work it together into a firm dough. Wrap in cling film and chill in the fridge for 30 minutes.

3 On a lightly floured work surface, roll the chilled pastry out to the size of a 20cm (8in) fluted flan tin. Prick it all over with a fork and put some greaseproof paper on top. Fill with baking beans and blind bake for about 20 minutes until it's a pale golden colour. Remove the paper and beans, then bake for a further 5 minutes. Remove from the oven. Reduce the heat to 130°C fan/150°C/gas 2.

4 For the filling, add the lemon juice and zest to a bowl along with the cornflour and mix together. Bring the water to the boil in a saucepan, then stir in your lemony cornflour mixture. Simmer gently, stirring continuously until it forms a thick custard-like consistency.

5 Beat the sugar and egg yolks in a separate bowl and thoroughly stir this into your custard. Bring back to the boil, whisking continuously until it just starts bubbling, then remove from the heat and allow to cool slightly. Pour it into your pastry case and spread evenly.

6 To make the meringue, whisk the egg whites on a high speed until they form stiff peaks. Now gradually add your caster sugar a spoonful at a time, whisking flat out between each addition. Heap your meringue over the top of the lemon filling and spread it out evenly, making sure there are no gaps. You can make wee swirly peaks at this point or whatever fancy idea comes to mind.

7 Bake for about 45 minutes, or until the meringue top is a crisp pale brown but nice and marshmallowy inside. You can serve this up warm or cold, so it really comes down to how hungry you are.

Pecan Pie

I got this recipe from my nanny as she always rants and raves about it. Better known as an American pudding, it has settled in as one of our family's favourites. It has a beautiful flaky and buttery shortcrust pastry, along with a caramel custard packed with nutty pecans. It's hard to beat with a cup of coffee. Soon, you too will be claiming it from America as your own, just like my nanny.

SERVES 8

300g pecans
1 x batch of Shortcrust Pastry (store-bought or see page 212)
plain flour, for dusting
4 eggs
125g soft dark brown sugar
1 tsp vanilla bean paste
125ml maple syrup
1 tsp lemon juice
good pinch of salt
50g butter, melted
50g dark chocolate, chopped

Loved by Alfie

'Great when I get it. Don't get it enough!'

1 Preheat the oven to 160°C fan/180°C/gas 4.

2 Spread the pecans out over a baking tray and toast in the oven for about 5 minutes, Remove and set aside 30 of these for decorating the top of your pie. Chop the rest.

3 Roll out your shortcrust pastry on a lightly floured surface to about 3mm thick and place this into a 23cm (9in) fluted tart tin. Use a piece of excess pastry to press the pastry into the edges of the tin. If there are any small tears or rips, you can patch these in with some of the excess pastry. Place a sheet of greaseproof paper on top of this and fill with your baking beans.

4 Bake for 20 minutes, or until the edges of the pastry shell are slightly golden. Remove the paper and baking beans, and bake for a further 5 minutes.

5 Remove from the oven and trim off any overhanging excess pastry with a knife. (My nanny will always have a wee taste test of the pastry and then crush the rest up and feed it to the birds in the garden.) Reduce the oven temperature to 150°C fan/170°C/gas 4.

6 For the filling, whisk together the eggs and brown sugar. Once combined, add the vanilla and maple syrup, whisking again. Add the lemon juice, salt and melted butter, and mix with a spatula. Finally, fold in the toasted chopped pecans and the dark chocolate.

7 Pour the filling into your prepared pastry shell and arrange the whole pecan nuts on top in any design you wish.

8 Bake for about 30–35 minutes until it has a slight wobble in the middle and is nicely browned on top.

9 Allow to cool fully before removing from the tin and slicing. This goes well with some freshly whipped cream or a big scoop of vanilla ice cream. I hope when you taste it you agree with my granda's verdict that you wouldn't get any better in a restaurant.

Chocolate Brioche Bread and Butter Pudding

Bread and butter pudding is a classic and this wee spin on it brings it up a level. We used to get bread and butter pudding at our Irish underage camps. I've never seen a bunch of young lads go more daft when they saw it. You'd literally inhale your dinner to ensure you got a healthy portion of this, swimming in custard. That might be the reason I spent most of my career in the front row!

SERVES 6

1 brioche loaf or bag of rolls, sliced (you can also use the chocolate chip ones if you fancy it)
butter, for greasing
150g raisins
200g chocolate of choice, chopped (or use chocolate chips)
500ml milk
50g white chocolate, chopped
zest of 1 orange
dash of vanilla extract
2 eggs
50g caster sugar

1. Layer a third of the brioche slices into a large greased baking dish (about 23cm/9in square). Sprinkle over half of the raisins and chocolate. Place another layer of brioche down (a third again), along with the rest of your raisins and chocolate. Add a final layer of brioche and move on to making the custard.
2. Heat the milk in a saucepan until it's almost simmering, stirring continuously. Add the white chocolate, orange zest and vanilla extract. Gently heat and stir until the chocolate has melted.
3. Whisk the eggs and sugar in a large bowl until well combined.
4. Bring the milk mixture to a simmer, stirring continuously, then remove from the heat. Add a third of it to the egg mixture and whisk well. Add it straight back into your saucepan of milk and cook over a low heat, stirring continuously, until a thin custard forms. This can take about 5 minutes.
5. Remove the custard from the heat and stir for another 2 minutes, then carefully pour it over the brioche pudding. You can use a fork to help it seep into the edges and wee crevices. Leave to soak for 15 minutes.
6. Preheat the oven to 160°C fan/180°C/gas 4.
7. Bake the pudding for about 40 minutes until the surface is a nice golden brown and the custard has just set.
8. Now all ye have to do is serve it up with latherings of custard.

Loved by Alfie

'Another one I don't get enough of!'

Vanilla Egg Custard Tarts

I'm torn between these and a pastel de nata for my favourite custard tart, but these hold a place in my heart from when I was younger. Mum loves these and would sometimes bring a few home from the Saturday shop. They would have been halved and shared evenly and always brought a smile to our faces. There's something so comforting about a soft-set custard and perfect contrast of the rich shortcrust pastry.

MAKES 12

- 1 x batch of Rich Shortcrust Pastry (store-bought or see page 213), chilled
- plain flour, for dusting
- 90g caster sugar
- 7 medium egg yolks, at room temperature
- 700ml whole milk
- ground or freshly grated nutmeg, for sprinkling

1 Preheat the oven to 180°C fan/200°C/gas 6.

2 Pop your chilled pastry onto a lightly floured work surface and roll out to about 5mm thick. Cut out 12 pastry discs with a 10–11cm floured pastry cutter (if you have a fluted one – great, but don't worry if not). Press these gently into your muffin tin. If you have any small tears, patch these up with any excess pastry. You want your pastry to come slightly over the top of each dip in the tin. Crimp the edges with a teaspoon or fork. Pop these into the fridge to chill and move onto your custard filling.

3 Add the sugar and egg yolks to a large bowl and whisk until pale and creamy. Gently heat the milk in a saucepan over a medium-high heat, whisking continuously until just before boiling. Gradually pour the milk into the egg yolk mixture, whisking continuously, until you have a smooth mixture with tiny bubbles. Transfer to a jug.

4 Pour the custard into your pastry shells and sprinkle the tops with a little nutmeg. Bake for 15 minutes, then reduce the temperature to 160°C fan/180°C/gas 4 and bake for a further 10 minutes. They will be done when the filling is slightly domed with a small wobble.

5 Allow the tarts to cool in the muffin tin for about 20–30 minutes before removing carefully and cooling on a wire cooling rack. Now you can enjoy these firm favourites.

Loved by Alfie

'These are very tasty now.'

15

Key Lime Pie

My nanny loves citrus flavours and this is a favourite of mine as well. It's very easy to rustle up if you're pushed for time – all the heavy lifting is done by the fridge as it sets. It's fresh and light, perfect for the sunnier months, but have it just once and you will probably want to eat it all year round.

SERVES 8

For the base
200g digestive biscuits (or oatmeal biscuits), finely crushed
75g butter
25g Demerara sugar

For the filling
1 x 397g tin of condensed milk
juice of 4 limes
zest of 2 limes
450ml double cream

1 For the base, blitz the biscuits in a food processor or crush finely in a bowl with a rolling pin.

2 Gently melt the butter in a saucepan over a low–medium heat.

3 Pour the melted butter into the crushed biscuits, stirring to combine, then add the sugar and mix well.

4 Add this mixture to a 23cm (9in) pie dish and press it firmly into the base. Place in the fridge and move onto your filling.

5 Add the condensed milk, lime juice and the majority of the lime zest (keep enough to scatter over the top when decorating) to a large mixing bowl and beat until combined. Pour in 300ml of the double cream and beat until well blended – it will thicken and begin to hold its shape.

6 Pour the filling over the prepared biscuit base and smooth the top. Chill in the fridge for about 3–4 hours

7 Whip the remaining cream and spread this on top, then scatter the reserved lime zest over. Slice it up and serve.

Pear and Almond Tart

This recipe is one of my nanny's favourites, so I had to include it. It's more of a decadent pudding and one you would rustle up for a special occasion. It's delicate but equally delicious. I feel it could be one of your favourites too, once you give it a try.

SERVES 8

1 x batch of Shortcrust Pastry (store-bought or see page 212)
plain flour, for dusting
butter, for greasing
300ml water
1 tbsp caster sugar
1 tbsp vanilla sugar
4 pears

For the pastry cream
2 eggs
30g caster sugar
10g plain flour
200ml whole milk
40g ground almonds
45g crème fraîche

1 Preheat the oven to 180°C fan/200°C/gas 6.

2 Roll out the pastry on a lightly floured work surface to about 5mm thick and place in a lightly greased 20–23cm (8–9in) fluted flan tin. Gently press the pastry into the tin, trimming off any excess pastry. If there are any small tears, patch them up with your excess pastry. Cover with some greaseproof paper and fill with baking beans.

3 Bake for 15 minutes, then remove the greaseproof paper and baking beans and bake for another 5 minutes. Remove from the oven and allow to cool fully. Trim the pastry edges when it has cooled slightly.

4 In a saucepan, bring the water to the boil and stir in the caster and vanilla sugars.

5 Meanwhile, peel the pears, cut in half and remove the cores. Gently place these into the boiling water and poach for about 15 minutes, or until they are tender when a sharp knife is inserted. Remove from the heat and allow the pears to cool in the liquid.

6 While the pears are poaching, make the pastry cream. Beat the eggs and caster sugar in a large bowl until combined, then stir in the flour until smooth.

7 Heat the milk in a pan until just before it boils. Pour half of the milk into the egg mixture, whisking continuously until well combined. Pour this mixture back into the pan and heat over a medium–low heat, whisking continuously until it thickens. This should only take a few minutes. Remove from the heat and add the ground almonds and crème fraîche, whisking until well combined. Leave to cool.

8 Pour the cooled pastry cream into the pastry shell and smooth out. Place the pears on top, either as is, or slice and fan out.

9 Bake for about 35 minutes until browning on top. Remove from the oven and allow to rest in the tin for a few minutes before removing to a wire cooling rack to cool completely.

10 Serve warm or cold with some crème fraîche or cream.

Banoffee Trifle

This recipe couldn't be easier. If I'm honest, you can't really call it baking – it's more like construction. It's ticking the boxes as a deconstructed cheesecake, but the addition of custard makes me say trifle. Depending on the size of your trifle bowl, you can adjust the quantities – but if there's loads leftover, trust me, it won't last long.

SERVES 6–8

400g digestive biscuits
150g unsalted butter
2 x 397g tins of caramel or dulce de leche
1 x 500g tub of ready-made custard
3 bananas, sliced
500ml double cream
100g chocolate of choice, either grated, finely chopped or chips

1. Blitz the digestive biscuits in a food processor or crush in a ziplock bag using a rolling pin. Don't worry if there's the odd chunk, this will add a bit of texture.
2. Gently melt the butter over a low heat, stirring occasionally. Tip the crushed digestives into this and stir until combined.
3. Add half of the biscuit mix to a medium-sized trifle bowl and gently press it in, but don't compact it too much, as you want it to be easily scooped out later. Ensure it covers the base and push it slightly up the edges as well.
4. Spread one tin of caramel carefully over the biscuit base until it is evenly covered.
5. Do the same with half of the custard and smooth it over the caramel layer.
6. Layer half of the banana slices on top (you can place a ring of bananas against the side of the bowl if you'd like to impress with your design) and spread half of the cream over the top.
7. Repeat those layers again, gently crumbling the second layer of biscuit rather than compacting it. Be gentle as you add each layer.
8. Sprinkle the chocolate on top, then get yourself a big old bowl and enjoy.

Tip

You can put your own spin on this easy dessert by adding your favourite nuts if you wish, or using half biscuit, half sponge, or even banana bread. If you would prefer to have a more traditional trifle you could use a light sponge for the base, like the one from my Festive Trifle (page 209), but I find the biscuits work better here for flavour and texture.

Rice Pudding

This is a warm sweet hug in a bowl and really winds back the years. My dad always talks about his mum making this as a sweet treat when they were younger on the farm. He always jokes about their house growing up, that if you didn't grab or take immediately you went hungry. But then again there could have been at least 10 hungry hallions living under the one roof at a time. He always made sure to be the first of those hallions to be served when this bowl of nostalgia was on the go.

SERVES 4

360ml cold water
140g pudding rice
70g caster sugar
¼ tsp salt
480ml whole milk
1 large egg, beaten
125–150g su tanas
1 tbsp unsalted butter
½ tsp vanilla extract

1. Bring the water to the boil in a saucepan. Add the rice and stir it in, then reduce the heat to low. Cover and simmer until the rice is tender and the water has been absorbed, this should take about 20 minutes.
2. Transfer the cooked rice to a clean saucepan along with the sugar, salt and three-quarters of the milk. Cook over a medium heat, stirring every so often so it doesn't stick to the bottom, for about 15 minutes until thick and creamy.
3. Add the remaining milk, beaten egg and dried fruit and stir well. Cook for a few more minutes, stirring continuously until you get your desired consistency. Some like it runnier, some like it thicker (I'm in the thicker camp). Remove from the heat and add the butter and vanilla, stirring until combined.
4. Serve and enjoy this nostalgic hug in a bowl.

Summer Fruit Roulade

I might cause controversy here, especially in my family, but I prefer a roulade to a pavlova! This one ticks all the boxes – it's lovely and delicate inside and has a slight chew on the edges. The fresh cream and fruit are the perfect accompaniment, and there's no better way to take advantage of fresh seasonal fruit. You can honestly use whatever fruit you would like here, but I feel like this is a winning combination. My Granda Alfie gave this 11/10, so you'll definitely want to give it a whirl.

SERVES 8

- 5 egg whites
- 275g caster sugar
- 300ml fresh whipping cream
- 175g strawberries, half chopped, half sliced
- 175g raspberries

1. Preheat the oven to 170°C fan/190°C/gas 5.
2. Ensure your mixing bowl is completely clean and dry before adding the egg whites. Whisk on a high speed for a few minutes to break the whites up – it will become white and frothy. Gradually add your sugar a tablespoon at a time, whisking for about 15–20 seconds before adding the next spoonful. Whisk until it firms up and has a lovely shine to it. Scrape down the base and sides of your bowl to ensure it's all combined, giving it one last whisk.
3. Pop the meringue into a lined 23 x 33cm (9 x 13in) Swiss roll tin and smooth it out evenly. Trail a fork from one end to the other to create a nice design – this will look the part once you have it rolled up.
4. Bake for about 25 minutes until it's nicely golden on top.
5. Place a layer of greaseproof paper on your work surface and carefully flip your meringue out onto this. Allow to cool for about 10 minutes, just to the point that it's no longer warm.
6. Meanwhile, whip the cream to soft peaks and prepare the fruit.
7. Spread a good layer of fresh cream over the cooled meringue, then scatter over a layer of strawberries and raspberries.
8. Slice a shallow crease about 4cm from one end of the meringue. With the help of the greaseproof paper, roll up the meringue from the scored end to form your roulade. Lift the greaseproof paper to begin your roll, but don't roll the paper inside the meringue, just use it as a guide.
9. Place the roulade onto your serving dish or board and dig in. You will thoroughly enjoy this one – it's a perfect summer dessert.

Loved by Alfie

'Ohhh, it's good.'

Celebration Bakes

Mum's Pavlova

I could talk about this one for a month of Sundays. Mum's pavlova is legendary in our family. This is hands-down my mum's best dessert and it's ridiculously light and moreish. My uncle John would go to war for it. We dropped one off to him for his birthday and surprisingly he allowed my auntie Sharon and two cousins Natasha and Kaitlin a slice. But he saved about a third of it for the next day after work. He arrived home and it was gone. Well, all hell broke loose, and I think my cousin Natasha is now out of the will. Mum always made one for our family friends the Kirks when they threw an aul get together. The dad Ivan would always make sure there was a good slab of it hidden from the party so he could have it the next day for his breakfast. That's how good this thing is. I hope you get hooked on it, just like us.

SERVES 8–10

6 egg whites
340g caster sugar
2 tbsp cornflour
1 tbsp white vinegar

To decorate
500ml whipping cream, whipped with 1 tbsp icing sugar
1 x tin of pear quarters, drained and sliced
1 x tin of mandarin oranges, drained
handful of strawberries, sliced
chocolate orange segments
crumbly chocolate bar (such as a Flake)

Loved by Alfie

'Another one I taught your mum!'

1 Preheat the oven to 150°C fan/170°C/gas 4. Cover a large baking sheet with kitchen foil.

2 Make sure your mixing bowl is perfectly clean and dry. Loosely whisk the egg whites for about a minute just to break them up, then crank the mixer up to full speed and gradually add the caster sugar a tablespoon at a time. The mixture will gradually grow in volume and become silky smooth with a lovely shine. Add the cornflour and vinegar, and keep mixing on full throttle.

3 Use a spatula to dollop it onto the baking sheet and shape it into a big circle, about 25cm in diameter and 7.5cm high.

4 Pop it into the oven and reduce the heat down to 100°C fan/120°C/gas ½. Bake for at least 1½ hours.

5 Transfer the pavlova to your serving plate and allow it to cool fully before getting stuck into decorating.

6 My mum is pretty handy at this, but honestly you can chuck on whatever you fancy. Spread a layer of whipped cream on top, keeping some to pipe on after. Mum would normally fan the pears in the middle and place the mandarin oranges in between. Then she would pipe some swirls of whipped cream around the edges and a big one in the middle. Pop the strawberries onto and between the swirls, along with segments of chocolate orange. Finally, crumble that chocolate bar over the top.

Strawberry Swiss Roll

I learnt this recipe from my nanny Mamie and it's perfect for those sunnier days. The sponge is so light, and with the fresh cream and strawberries it's perfect to enjoy after a summer barbecue. I'd be lying if I said we didn't have this year-round. It's one of my mum's favourites – I think because it transports her back to her own granny's kitchen. Just as many of these recipes do to me. You can also switch up the fruit you use. We have strawberries in our vegetable garden so it's always a shame not to use them for something special like this.

SERVES 8

4 eggs, at room temperature
100g caster sugar, plus extra for sprinkling
100g self-raising flour, sifted
500ml double cream, whipped
large punnet of fresh strawberries, some sliced and some chopped
crumbly chocolate bar (such as a Flake)

1 Preheat the oven to 200°C fan/220°C/gas 7. Line a 23 x 33cm (9 x 13in) Swiss roll tin with greaseproof paper.

2 Whisk the eggs in a mixing bowl for a few minutes on a medium speed to get them broken up. Crank up the speed and continue to whisk, adding the caster sugar gradually. Whisk away until it becomes light and frothy, then give the bottom and sides of the bowl a scrape with a spatula. Whisk again for a few more minutes.

3 Sift in half of the flour and fold it in very carefully. You want it to hold all the air pockets you have created. My nanny always uses a beater from her hand mixer for this.

4 Add the second half of the flour and when it's fully incorporated, gently pour the mixture into the tin. Spread it out evenly with a spatula, but be gentle with it, it's delicate.

5 Bake for 10 minutes, or until it is golden brown and starting to shrink from the edges of the tin.

6 Dust some greaseproof paper with caster sugar and turn your sponge out onto this. Remove the greaseproof paper that you baked your sponge on. Press into the sponge an inch from one end using a palette knife or something similar. You don't want to cut it through, just make a nice divot or score mark. Roll the sponge up from that end, using your greaseproof paper to help when you get started. You don't want the greaseproof paper lodged in the middle of it, it's just to help keep the caster sugar on and keep things tidy. Leave to cool fully.

Loved by Alfie

'Sweet and tasty.'

7 When cool, roll the sponge back out on the greaseproof paper. Spread a layer of whipped cream over the sponge (you can also spread some jam over the sponge before this, but we prefer it without). Top the cream with a layer of sliced strawberries, then roll the sponge back up tightly.

8 We like to spread and pipe some more cream on top, chuck on some chopped strawberries to decorate, then finally crumble that flaky chocolate bar over the top. This wee roll of joy is so light you could polish it off by yourself. But try to share, because no one likes a greedy sow.

Jelly Ring

This one is a blast from the past and always made an appearance for Sunday dessert. It's nothing fancy, but it floods nostalgia for a lot of locals here at home. With a lovely light sponge, cream and jelly, what's not to love. It's perfect for kids (probably the reason for the nostalgia), but trust me no grown-ups will be turning this wee gem down.

SERVES 6

1 x 135g packet of raspberry jelly
3 eggs
85g caster sugar
85g self-raising flour
Raspberry Jam (store-bought or see page 215)
125ml fresh whipping cream, whipped
desiccated coconut, for sprinkling

1 First, make up your jelly by following the instructions on the packet. Allow this to partially set in the fridge. You can pop it into the freezer, but make sure to keep an eye on it and stir every 20–30 minutes.

2 Preheat the oven to 160°C fan/180°C/gas 4. Line a 25cm (10in) ring tin with greaseproof paper.

3 For your sponge, whisk the eggs in a mixing bowl on a high speed for a few minutes until they froth up. Gradually add the sugar, a tablespoon at a time, while you continue to whisk. The mixture will grow in volume, becoming smooth, light and airy.

4 Gradually sift in the self-raising flour, gently folding this in between each addition. Do this until all the flour is fully combined.

5 Pour the batter into your tin and bake for 20–25 minutes until lightly golden and springy to the touch. Remove from the tin while it's still warm (run a knife around the sides to help you do this). Allow to cool fully on a wire cooling rack.

6 Meanwhile, wash and dry the ring tin.

7 When cooled, slice your sponge in half and spread a layer of raspberry jam on the top side. Spread a decent layer of whipped cream on the base and sandwich these back together.

8 Pour your partially set jelly into your cleaned ring tin and place the sponge on top. Press this in gently at first, then firmly to allow the jelly to surround the sponge. Wrap in some cling film and allow to set in the fridge for about 4–6 hours until the jelly is firm.

9 Once set, briefly dip the tin in some warm water to allow the jelly ring to come out easily. Place a plate on top and and flip the tin over to remove. Sprinkle with some desiccated coconut and serve it up.

Hazelnut Chocolate Tiramisu

I made this for a special person's birthday and it was loved by everyone. I had to include it in the book. Tiramisu is the coffee lover's dessert, but if you don't like coffee or want to avoid the alcohol that's generally in tiramisu, this is the one. It takes very little effort, but looks impressive, as if you'd slaved over it for a day. It is moist, light and chocolatey, and will have you going back for another bowl, trust me.

SERVES 10

500g mascarpone
250g hazelnut chocolate spread
3 tbsp icing sugar
1 tsp vanilla extract
500ml double cream
400–500g sponge fingers
500ml double cream, to pipe on top (optional)
cocoa powder, for dusting

For the soaking liquid
400ml milk of choice
1½ tbsp icing sugar
1½ tbsp cocoa powder

1. Start with the soaking liquid. Heat the milk until tepid in a saucepan or the microwave, then add the icing sugar and cocoa powder, whisking until combined. Heating the milk will make it easier to combine. Set aside.
2. Add the mascarpone and hazelnut chocolate spread to a separate large mixing bowl. Beat these together until smooth, then add the icing sugar, vanilla extract and double cream. Beat again until it just thickens to a creamy, pale chocolatey mixture. Be careful not to overmix it or it will go lumpy and look curdled.
3. Soak the sponge fingers in the chocolatey milk for a few seconds on each side, until they absorb some of the liquid. Do this in a few batches so they don't get saturated – you want them to have a little texture. Arrange a layer of these on the base of a deep serving dish.
4. Scoop half of your smooth hazelnut cream mixture on top and smooth it out evenly.
5. Repeat steps 3 and 4 again, then pop it into the fridge for about 3 hours to set, or overnight if you can bear to wait.
6. If you're feeling fancy, whip some fresh cream and pipe it over the top in any design you wish. I find little blobs or mounds of cream look great, especially when you give them a dusting of cocoa powder. Now get yourself a big bowlful and dig in. The special person that inspired this dessert loved it and I hope you enjoy it just as much!

Honeycomb Cheesecake

This is another recipe I inherited from Mum. It's simple, but extremely effective. I always rustle this up for a special occasion, whether it's a birthday party, barbecue or any get together. The beauty is, it tastes even better the next day. The honeycomb starts to melt through the cheesecake and adds even more flavour. It might not have the same honeycomb crunch – it's almost chewy – but anyone that's had it prefers it the next day. The only issue is trying to constrain yourself from digging in. Or do what my dad does – save a slice for breakfast the day after the party.

SERVES 8–10

100g salted butter
300g digestive biscuits
400g full-fat cream cheese
100g icing sugar
8 bars of chocolate-covered honeycomb (such as Crunchie bars)
250ml double cream

To decorate
150ml double cream
2 tbsp icing sugar
your preferred chocolate, broken up or grated

Loved by Alfie

'Lovely and sweet.'

1 Melt the butter in a pan over a low–medium heat. Set aside.

2 Finely crush the digestive biscuits in a food processor or with a rolling pin in a bowl. Add the melted butter and stir to combine.

3 Add the biscuit base mixture to a 20cm (8in) loose-bottomed cake tin and press it firmly in. (It's optional, but you can bake the base – it makes it nice and crispy. If so, bake at 170°C fan/190°C/gas 5 for 5–10 minutes, then set aside to fully cool.)

4 For the filling, add the cream cheese to a mixing bowl and sift in the icing sugar. Beat until they are combined and smooth.

5 Using the end of a rolling pin, bash your unopened chocolate honeycomb bars from one end to the other. Do this on the flat side and then what would be the edge of the bar – this will give you a range of nice chunks of honeycomb and some honeycomb dust. Open the packets and add the honeycomb rubble to the cream cheese mixture, folding together until combined.

6 In a separate bowl, whip the cream, then add this to the honeycomb mixture. Gently fold to combine. Dollop the mixture on top of your cooled biscuit base, pressing it right to the bottom and smoothing the top. Cover with some cling film and allow to set in the fridge for about 6 hours, or overnight if you can resist.

7 Remove from the tin and place on a serving plate. To decorate, whip the cream and icing sugar together and add to a piping bag. Pipe swirls on top in any fashion you like. Decorate with your preferred chocolate – whether that's chunks, grating it or just wee mini bars, go wild and put your own spin on it. Now for the best part – get yourself a big slice and enjoy!

Hot Cross Buns

These will always be a favourite at Easter, but once you make your own, you'll more than likely be having them all the time. They're full of flavour from the spice and are extremely fluffy and soft. These need to be eaten on the day of making, but they'll probably last not much longer as soon as you dig in.

MAKES 12

640g strong bread flour, plus extra for dusting
110g caster sugar
2 tsp ground cinnamon
2 tsp allspice or mixed spice
½ tsp salt
9g (3 tsp) instant dried (fast-action) yeast
210g sultanas
zest of 1–2 oranges
375ml milk, warmed
1 egg, beaten
50g butter, melted and cooled
vegetable oil, for greasing

For the crosses
75g plain flour
about 6 tbsp water

For the glaze
2 tbsp apricot jam
4 tbsp water

1 Add the flour, sugar, cinnamon, allspice, salt and yeast to a stand mixer fitted with a dough hook and mix well (or use a large mixing bowl and give it a light mix with a spoon).

2 Add the sultanas, orange zest, milk, egg and melted butter. If you're using your hands to knead, bring it all together in your bowl using a spoon or fork, then knead for about 10 minutes until it's nice and smooth and stretchy. It will take about 5 minutes in a stand mixer.

3 Gently shape into a ball, pop into a bowl and cover with some cling film. Leave it in a warmish spot for about 30 minutes–1 hour until it doubles in size.

4 Gently punch the air out of your dough and pop it onto a lightly floured surface. Roll into a log, then cut into 12 equal pieces. Flatten each with the palm of your hand, bring each side into the middle and pinch together, then roll into a nice smooth ball. Place these, seam-side down, onto a 23 x 30cm (9 x 12in) baking tray lined with greaseproof paper with some overhang.

5 Loosely cover with some lightly oiled cling film and leave to prove for about 40 minutes. Once they have risen to about 1½ times their original size, they are good to go.

6 Preheat the oven to 160°C fan/180°C/gas 4.

7 Mix the flour and water until it's smooth to give a thick and runny paste and place in a small piping bag. Pipe this over your dough to create your crosses

8 Bake for about 20–25 minutes until they're a deep golden brown on top. Using the overhang of greaseproof paper, remove from the tray and place on a wire cooling rack.

9 Heat the apricot jam and water in a saucepan, then brush this all over your hot cross buns while they are still warm. Allow them to cool a little before getting stuck in. Ripping one of these open when slightly warm and plastering it in butter is hard to beat.

Mince Pies Topped with Almond Meringue

Nanny Mamie's mince pies are legendary around our parts. Well, in my head they are. I did a small Christmas fair in Galway a few years ago and she helped me by making a good few batches. People came back the next day for more and wanted to put orders in. Unfortunately, I wasn't the brains behind them, but I'm slowly mastering them. This is a twist on her usual recipe, but they're equally tasty.

MAKES 24

For the pastry

200g plain flour, plus extra for dusting

75g unsalted butter, cubed

30g lard or Trex/vegetable fat, cubed

zest of 1 orange

3 tbsp cold water

For the filling

250g mincemeat (store-bought is perfect)

1 pear, grated

For the almond meringue topping

3 egg whites

300g icing sugar

4 tsp vanilla bean paste

300g ground almonds

1 Preheat the oven to 160°C fan/180°C/gas 4.

2 Add the flour, butter and lard to a food processor and blitz until combined. You can also do this by working it through your fingertips, but the food processor makes life that bit easier. Pop in the orange zest and give it another quick blitz before finally adding the water and blitzing again. Once it starts to form into lumps, it's ready.

3 Transfer the mixture to a bowl and bring it together into a ball using your hands. Pop it onto a lightly floured surface and roll it out to about 2mm thick. Using a 6cm pastry cutter or glass, cut out your pastry shells and place them in your bun tray/patty tin.

4 For the filling, mix the mincemeat and grated pear in a bowl.

5 For the almond meringue, whisk the egg whites in a spotlessly clean bowl until they are stiff. Gradually add the icing sugar, whisking between additions. Once this becomes nice and silky, almost glossy, add the vanilla bean paste. Give it another whisk with the mixer, then add the ground almonds in 3 or 4 stages, mixing them through until fully combined. Transfer the mixture to a piping bag.

6 Spoon a heaped teaspoon of the mincemeat mixture into each pastry shell, then pipe a nice wee swirl of meringue on top.

7 Bake for about 35 minutes until the tops turn golden. Allow them to cool in the tin for 10 minutes before transferring them to a wire rack to cool fully.

8 These are actually nicer the next day. The meringue top gets slightly chewier and just tastes better. If you can resist, leave them overnight. You can always sample just the one (but that's never the case).

Christmas Cake

This recipe is my great grandmother's. She was known for making Christmas cakes and giving them out to family and friends every year. My nanny has kept the tradition up and still uses her recipe and method today. This cake is bursting with flavour, rich and tasty with all the juicy fruit and brandy. Make it 6–8 weeks before the big day to feed it its diet of brandy and allow the flavour to mature. It's well worth the effort and makes a thoughtful gift for anyone close to you.

SERVES 12 WITH MULTIPLE SLICES

225g salted butter, softened
225g dark muscovado sugar
50g mixed candied peel, finely chopped
100g dried apricots, chopped
grated zest of 1 lemon
grated zest of 1 orange
50g finely chopped almonds
1 tbsp black treacle
225g plain flour
¼ tsp ground nutmeg
½ tsp mixed spice
4 eggs, lightly beaten
1–2 tbsp brandy, for feeding (optional)

For the overnight soak

170g currants
225g sultanas
225g raisins
100g glacé cherries, rinsed, dried and quartered
3 tbsp brandy

1 The night before you plan to make this, put the dried fruit in for an overnight soak. Combine the currants, sultanas, raisins and glacé cherries in a bowl and sprinkle over the brandy. Cover with a clean tea towel and leave overnight.

2 The next day, add the butter and sugar to a large mixing bowl and beat well.

3 Add the candied peel, apricots, lemon and orange zests and chopped almonds to your soaked fruit and mix well.

4 Scrape down the base and sides of your bowl to ensure the butter and sugar is combined fully, then add the treacle and continue beating until it's nice and creamy.

5 In a separate bowl, combine the flour, nutmeg and mixed spice, giving this a mix with a spoon. Add this to the butter and sugar mixture along with the beaten eggs, slowly beating until fully combined.

6 Gradually add the fruit mixture to the batter, folding it in in stages until the fruit is evenly distributed.

7 Line the base and sides of a 20cm (8in) cake tin, at least 7.5cm (3in) deep, with greaseproof paper. Spoon the batter into the tin, smooth it out and create a little dent in the middle. You can also wrap a strip of cardboard around the outside of the tin and secure it with some fine wire or kitchen string (but this is optional). Cut two circles of greaseproof paper to the size of the tin and snip a 2.5cm hole in the middle of each. Loosely place over the top of the batter

To decorate
2 tbsp apricot jam
icing sugar, for dusting
ready-to-roll marzipan
ready-to-roll fondant icing
extra brandy, for brushing
Christmas decorations and ribbon of your choice

8 The secret to a good Christmas cake is a low and slow bake in the oven. Preheat the oven to 120°C fan/140°C/gas 1 and bake the cake for about 4 hours.

9 Allow it to cool fully in the tin before taking out and removing the greaseproof paper.

10 Store the cake in a tin and feed it with 1–2 tablespoons of brandy 2 weeks before decorating to allow the surface to dry before icing. (You can leave out this feeding stage but it adds more flavour to the cake and keeps it moist. We only feed it once, as otherwise it gets too soggy.)

11 Now it's time to decorate. Gently heat the apricot jam in a saucepan over a low heat, then brush it over the top of your cake. Dust the work surface with some icing sugar and roll out your marzipan and icing to a little larger than the size of your cake. Flip the apricot-coated top of your cake onto the marzipan and cut around it with a knife. Turn it the right-side up and lightly wash the top of the marzipan with brandy. Repeat the process to top with the icing layer. Now you can put your own Christmas twist on the decorations. My nanny always puts a nice design around the edges of the icing and adds Christmas decorations she has acquired over the years. You will be delighted with all the effort put into this cake. Especially over the Christmas Holidays when you gift it or enjoy with a cup of tea with family and friends.

Loved by Alfie

'Mamie's mother always made these and it's a great memory.'

Lemon Meringue Biscuits

Christmas Pudding

This is far from the dense, tar-like pudding you get in the shops. It is light and delicate, packed with juicy plump fruit, and is my favourite Christmas dessert. The recipe makes several small puddings and one large pudding, so the whole family gets one. You can halve the mixture if you'd prefer fewer. You can make these a month in advance to allow the flavour to mature, but you can also have them straight away. We use 450ml (1lb) foil pudding bowls for the smaller puddings and a large 1.2 litre (2 pint) plastic bowl for the family pudding.

MAKES 1 LARGE AND 7 SMALL PUDDINGS

225g sultanas
225g raisins
225g currants
225g Bramley apple, grated
grated zest of 1 orange
grated zest of 1 lemon
1 tsp salt
285ml Guinness
100ml brandy
450g brown sugar
450g salted butter, softened
170g plain flour
½ tsp ground nutmeg
½ tsp ground cinnamon
½ tsp mixed spice
½ tsp ground cloves
6 eggs, lightly beaten
340g fresh breadcrumbs

1 The night before you plan to make this, put the fruit mixture in for an overnight soak. Combine the dried fruits, apple, zests and salt in a suitable bowl and leave to soak in the Guinness and brandy. Cover with a clean tea towel and leave overnight.

2 The next day, give the fruit mixture a mix to wake it up.

3 Beat the brown sugar and butter in a stand mixer until it becomes smooth and creamy. This can take up to 10 minutes as you want it fully incorporated and smooth. Make sure to scrape the base and sides of the bowl every few minutes.

4 In a separate bowl, combine the flour and spices with a spoon. Gradually add to the butter and sugar mixture, along with the eggs, continuing to beat. Once this is fully combined, gradually add the breadcrumbs and mix well.

5 Add the soaked fruit in stages, folding it through the mixture.

6 Divide among your foil pudding cases and larger pudding bowl (if using) and seal with the lids.

7 Steam the puddings for 1½–2 hours (see note), or until the tops are firm when you remove the lids. Remove from the steamer (carefully) and allow them to cool fully.

8 Store in a cool dry place (or in the fridge, if you have room). To serve, reheat them on the big day. You can do this in a pan of simmering water, or even just scoop some into a bowl and microwave. Now the difficult part – custard, fresh cream or ice cream?

Note

We use an electric steamer with 3 levels to steam all the small puddings together. The larger pudding is steamed on its own. Alternatively, place the puddings on top of a saucer in a large pan of simmering water, ensuring the water comes at least halfway up the side of the pudding bowls.

Granny Margaret's Apple Sponge

This dessert transports me back to when Granny Margaret and Granda Billy would have thrown Halloween, Boxing Day and New Year's Eve parties. It has a special place in my heart with some great memories. Granny Margaret would just throw a bit of this and a bit of that in, just knowing instinctively what the required amount was. It's such a simple dessert but so delicious, especially when covered in some warm Vanilla Custard (see page 217).

SERVES 8

For the filling

- 2 large Bramley apples (about 500g), peeled, cored and roughly chopped into chunks
- 2 tbsp water
- 1 tbsp lemon juice
- 20g salted butter
- 2 tbsp caster sugar

For the topping

- 75g salted butter
- 100g caster sugar
- 2 eggs, lightly beaten
- 100g self-raising flour, sifted
- 75–100g sultanas (optional)
- 1 tbsp boiling water

1. Preheat the oven to 160°C fan/180°C/gas 4.
2. For the filling, place the apples in a saucepan along with the water and lemon juice. Stir together and cook over a medium for about 5 minutes until the apples have softened, but you don't want them to stew and become mushy.
3. Add the butter and caster sugar, then stir until fully combined and the sugar has dissolved. Transfer to a deep baking dish, about 14 x 20cm (5 x 8in), and leave to cool while you make the topping.
4. Cream the butter and caster sugar until pale and fluffy, scraping the bottom and sides of the bowl to ensure it's fully combined. Add a few tablespoons of the beaten eggs and fold in with a spatula, then do the same with the flour. Repeat this until you have used both up and the mixture is smooth and fully combined. Be sure to fold rather than beat, as this will help to keep air in the mixture and give a nice light sponge top. Add the sultanas and boiling water to the mix and gentle fold through.
5. Gently spoon the topping over the apple filling and smooth the top.
6. Bake for about 30–35 minutes until the top is golden and puffy, and an inserted skewer in the sponge comes out clean.
7. Allow to cool for about 10 minutes, then scoop into bowls with some fresh custard or whipped cream.

Profiteroles

These are my little sister's favourite dessert, to the point she has her own separate batch on Christmas Day. If you're lucky, you get one, but it's a rare sight even during the season of giving. They're a classic dessert that sometimes gets overlooked, but a stack of these dripping with chocolate sauce are hard to look past.

MAKES 24

- vegetable oil, for greasing
- 1 x batch of Choux Pastry (see page 214)
- 300ml double cream
- 200g milk chocolate, broken up
- 25g salted butter
- 25g golden syrup

1. Preheat the oven to 200°C fan/220°C/gas 7. Lightly brush 2 baking sheets with oil.
2. Make your choux pastry according to the instructions on page 214 and spoon into a piping bag. Pipe walnut-sized rounds of pastry onto your baking sheets, setting them well apart to allow them space to expand.
3. Bake for 15–20 minutes until risen, golden and crisp. Remove them from the oven and use a teaspoon to make a wee hole in the base of each bun (this allows the steam to escape). Pop them back into the oven for another 2 minutes to crisp a little more. Transfer to a wire cooling rack to cool fully.
4. Add 6 tablespoons of the cream to a small saucepan and set it aside. Whip the remainder in a separate bowl. Transfer the whipped cream to a piping bag and pipe it through the hole in the base of the buns (alternatively, you can split them and spread with cream). Place them on a serving plate and set aside.
5. Add the chocolate, butter and syrup to the cream in the pan. Melt this gently over a medium heat, stirring occasionally. Once melted and combined, and before serving, pour over your profiteroles or transfer the chocolate to a piping bag and pipe the tops individually. Now get stuck in, enjoying these wee mouthfuls of light and delicious joy. Make sure to share (unlike my sister Emma, who could easily have the lot)!

Festive Trifle

This trifle is rustled up every Christmas and even at Easter in our house. It's hard to call it a recipe, because it's more an assembly of convenient ingredients. But it will remind you of the trifle your nanny would have made (probably because it actually is a recipe from a nanny). It's the perfect nostalgic dessert, if you ask me, taking you back to the days of jelly and ice cream.

SERVES 8

1 plain Swiss roll sponge (store-bought or use the sponge from page 188) or a store-bought raspberry Swiss roll with no cream
Raspberry Jam (store-bought or see page 215)
1 x 300g tin of raspberries, drained
1 x 415g tin of fruit cocktail, drained
1 x 135g packet of raspberry jelly
600ml Vanilla Custard (store-bought fresh or powdered, or see page 217 – see tip, below)
500ml double cream, softly whipped

To decorate
chocolate of choice, for grating or breaking into shards
fresh cherries (optional)

1 If you're using the Swiss roll sponge or any plain sponge, rip it into 5cm chunks. Spread some raspberry jam on each piece and layer them in your trifle bowl. If you're using a store-bought jam Swiss roll, cut it into 3cm slices and layer in your trifle bowl.

2 Add the raspberries to the bowl, then layer the fruit cocktail on top.

3 Make up your jelly mixture according to the packet instructions, then pour it over the contents of the trifle bowl, giving it a bit of a shake to allow it to seep through. Pop the bowl into the fridge to set.

4 Meanwhile, make your custard (if not using store-bought) and allow it to cool fully in the fridge.

5 Once your jelly is set, give the custard a good mix and add it to the trifle bowl. Smooth the top and pop it back into the fridge for about 30 minutes to firm up.

6 Once your custard has firmed up, top with the whipped cream (you probably won't need it all – some will be left over to serve it with). Grate or crumble over your preferred chocolate and add a few cherries to decorate (if you wish). Now get yourself a big old bowl of this and dig in!

Tip

Store-bought fresh custard won't set as well as powdered or homemade but does save time.

Homemade Basics

Shortcrust Pastry

This simple shortcrust pastry recipe will be your right-hand man from now on. Whether you're making a classic tart or one of the many wee bun recipes in this book, you'll be whipping this up. You can use it in so many ways. You'll notice that as you work through the book, I try to be as normal and straight as ever. No point frilling things up and acting like I'm something I'm not. I'm still the same lad from a wee village in the sticks that loves baking and learning our traditions from his nanny.

For a rough guide, these amounts will make you a decent-sized tart. You're talkin' a large (ovenproof) dinner plate. That's what I use when making any of my tarts and it's just as good as any fancy gear out there!

MAKES 370G

225g plain flour
pinch of salt
85g unsalted butter
55g Trex (white vegetable fat)
2 tbsp cold water

1 You can make this by hand or in a food processor. Add the plain flour and salt to your bowl or food processor, along with the butter and vegetable fat. Blitz this together or use your fingertips to rub the fats into the flour. Once it's combined it will look a bit like dry breadcrumbs.

2 Now add the cold water and blitz or work it through with your hands until it starts to hold its shape.

3 Pop the pastry into a bowl (or keep it in the one you're using) and bring it all together. Form into a ball and wrap in some cling film. Chill it in the fridge for about 45 minutes–1 hour before using.

Tip

You can make a big batch of this and freeze it for whenever you need it. Defrost overnight in the fridge or remove from the freezer in the morning to use in the afternoon.

Rich Shortcrust Pastry

This pastry is perfect for the likes of an Apple Cream (page 80) or Jonny's Wee Raspberry Tarts (see page 147) – you know the type of wee buns I'm talking about. It's sweeter than the regular shortcrust and perfect for making pastry shells. And there's plenty of other recipes out there that this pastry will suit perfectly.

MAKES ABOUT 330G

110g margarine, softened (if you like, you can swap in a percentage of butter as well)
40g caster sugar
2 tsp whole milk
175g plain flour
pinch of salt

1. In a bowl, cream the margarine and sugar together until pale and fluffy.
2. Add the milk and beat until combined.
3. Gradually sift in the flour and salt, slowly beating it all in.
4. Once combined, bring together with your hands to form a smooth dough ball. Wrap in cling film and chill in the fridge for 1 hour before using.

Tip

You can also make a big batch of this and freeze it for whenever you need it. Defrost overnight in the fridge or remove from the freezer in the morning to use in the afternoon.

Choux Pastry

This pastry is surprisingly easy to make and is perfect for your profiterole and éclair recipes (see pages 206 and 148). Those are the two classics that come to mind with this stuff, but honestly you can fill this pastry with whatever you like. You aren't just bound to sweet fillings either – it may surprise you how good a wee savoury option is (try cream cheese and chive; creamy mushroom; creamy goat's cheese and onion marmalade; smoked salmon and cream cheese).

MAKES ENOUGH FOR 6–8 ÉCLAIRS OR 24 PROFITEROLES

70g plain flour
55g salted butter
150ml water
2 eggs, beaten

1 Sift the flour onto a sheet of greaseproof paper and set aside.

2 Add the butter and water to a saucepan and gently melt over a medium–low heat, stirring occasionally. Now bring this to the boil, then remove from the heat.

3 Quickly add your flour to the saucepan by creasing the greaseproof paper and shooting it in. Beat vigorously with a wooden spoon until it comes together and forms a dough.

4 Pop the pan back onto the heat, continuously beating until the mixture forms a smooth, shiny ball and comes away from the sides of the pan. Remove from the heat and leave to cool for 2–3 minutes.

5 Gradually add the eggs to the dough, continuously beating until you have a smooth, stiff, shiny paste. If you reach this consistency and still have a little egg left, don't worry. Now your choux pastry is ready to use.

Homemade Jam

I helped my nanny make homemade jam all the time as a young lad and I still do today. If you've never made your own jam, this is your sign to start. As much as I rave about homemade things tasting better, the stuff from the shop bears no comparison to this. You really taste the fruit in this and it's as natural as it can get. It's that good my little sister Emma refuses to eat any other jam now.

MAKES 7–8 JARS

900g raspberries (or strawberries)
(2 tbsp lemon juice, if making strawberry jam)
900g jam sugar

1 First make sure your raspberries are washed. If there are any bruised or off-looking ones, discard them. Pop the raspberries into a heavy-based pan (we always use our big soup pot for this) and bring to the boil, stirring every so often.

2 Meanwhile, you can sterilise your jam jars. Wash them thoroughly and place them on a baking tray in 120°C fan/140°C/gas 1 oven for about 10 minutes. Place a saucer in the fridge to get cold.

3 Once the raspberries have come to the boil, gradually add your jam sugar, stirring after each addition and letting it dissolve before adding more. Once you've added all the sugar, simmer for about 10 minutes.

4 Remove the pan from the heat and test the jam for a set. To do this, put a small amount on the cold saucer. If it starts to wrinkle and set, you're good to go. If not, give it another 5 minutes and test again.

5 Once ready, remove your sterilised jam jars from the oven. Pour your jam into a measuring jug, then pour it into your jars.

6 Pop a waxed paper disc on top of each jar and seal with some cellophane discs and an elastic band. You can pick up these wee jam kits online or in a local home store. Allow the jars to cool enough before screwing on the lids tightly.

7 Leave to cool fully, then store in a cool dry place. This jam will last well over 6 months if unopened and when you crack one open, keep it in the fridge. You won't look back when you start making your own jam. It's a very thoughtful gift, if you can bring yourself to give it away.

For Strawberry Jam

Use the same quantities as above. Chop your strawberries up and when boiling, squish them against the side of your pot with the back of your wooden spoon to break up any big lumps. Add the lemon juice after simmering for 10 minutes. Add your jam sugar as above, bring back up to the boil and simmer for another 5 minutes, continuously stirring. While doing this, skim off any scum on the surface and discard it. Follow the rest of the method above.

Cream Cheese Frosting

Here's a simple recipe for the creamiest cream cheese frosting you'll ever have. Perfect for a Carrot Cake (page 99) or to lather all over your Cinnamon Buns (page 134), the options are endless if you're a fan of this stuff.

MAKES ENOUGH TO ICE 1 CAKE OR 1 BATCH OF CINNAMON BUNS

225g cream cheese
115g unsalted butter, softened
240g icing sugar
1 tsp vanilla extract

1. Add the cream cheese to a bowl and beat until smooth.
2. Add the softened butter and beat again until combined and smooth. Scrape down the sides midway through, to ensure it's fully combined.
3. Sift in your icing sugar and pour in your vanilla extract. Beat again, but start on a low speed so you don't plaster the kitchen in icing sugar. Slowly build up the speed as it combines until it's smooth and fully incorporated.
4. Cover and place in the fridge until you're ready to frost your desired bakes.

Vanilla Custard

We all need a go-to custard recipe, whether it's to slather over a fresh slice of apple tart, a crumble or even a wee slice of plain cake. This recipe is simple and has that lovely smooth vanilla flavour we all love. So instead of running to the shop, rustle up this delicious recipe instead.

MAKES ABOUT 700ML

1 vanilla pod
600ml whole milk (you can substitute some milk for double cream if you would like a richer, creamier custard)
4 large egg yolks
2 tbsp caster sugar
1 tbsp cornflour

1 Halve your vanilla pod and scrape out the seeds. Add both to a saucepan with the milk and bring it just to the boil over a medium heat, stirring regularly. Remove from the heat, cover and leave to rest for 20 minutes. This will allow the vanilla to infuse further, but remember to take out your vanilla pod after this time.

2 Add the egg yolks, sugar and cornflour to a large mixing bowl and whisk until combined and pale. Gradually pour your warm milk into the bowl, a little at a time, whisking well after each addition until you've added it all.

3 Pour this mixture back into your saucepan, place over a low heat and gently cook for about 20 minutes. You need to continuously whisk this and it will gradually start to thicken. Once you have reached your desired consistency, pour over the delicious dessert you have lined up.

4 If not using straight away, once cooled, you can store it in the fridge in a sealed container for 2–3 days.

Index

Conversion Tables

Recipes have been tested using metric measurements. Imperial conversions may yield different results. Follow one set of measurements only – do not mix metric and imperial.

WEIGHT

METRIC	IMPERIAL
15g	½ oz
25g	1 oz
40g	1½ oz
50g	2 oz
75g	3 oz
100g	4 oz
150g	5 oz
175g	6 oz
200g	7 oz
225g	8 oz
250g	9 oz
275g	10 oz
350g	12 oz
375g	13 oz
400g	14 oz
425g	15 oz
450g	1 lb
550g	1¼ lb
675g	1½ lb
900g	2 lb
1.5kg	3 lb

VOLUME

METRIC	IMPERIAL
25ml	1 fl oz
50ml	2 fl oz
85ml	3 fl oz
150ml	5 fl oz (¼ pint)
300ml	10 fl oz (½ pint)
450ml	15 fl oz (¾ pint)
600ml	1 pint
700ml	1¼ pints
900ml	1½ pints
1 litre	1¾ pints
1.2 litres	2 pints
1.25 litres	2¼ pints
1.5 litres	2½ pints
1.6 litres	2¾ pints
1.75 litres	3 pints
1.8 litres	3¼ pints
2 litres	3½ pints
2.1 litres	3¾ pints
2.25 litres	4 pints
2.75 litres	5 pints

MEASUREMENTS

METRIC	IMPERIAL
0.5cm	¼ inch
1cm	½ inch
2.5cm	1 inch
5cm	2 inches
5cm	3 inches
10cm	4 inches
15cm	6 inches
18cm	7 inches
20cm	8 inches
23cm	9 inches
25cm	10 inches
30cm	12 inches

OVEN TEMPERATURES

°C (NON FAN)	°F
140°C	275°F
150°C	300°F
160°C	325°F
180°C	350°F
190°C	375°F
200°C	400°F
220°C	425°F
230°C	450°F
240°C	475°F

Dedication

I never once thought I would be writing a book. Other than striving to be a professional rugby player, I never knew what I wanted to do with my life. I still don't know what that thing is, but I've learnt over the years that all I want to achieve is happiness. May that be by baking and cooking with my loved ones and sharing it with you all online or putting these loved recipes into cookbooks. It doesn't matter what you do and it shouldn't matter to anyone else. If you are happy and are enjoying the life you have created, that's all that matters. Just be sure to share it with the ones you love, because the memories you will make are hands-down the best part of the whole journey.

With that in mind, I want to dedicate this entire book and journey to all those who have helped me through life. To my parents, who would walk through hell on earth for me. My little sister, who is more like a best friend, even though she's probably sick of all my questions and requests for advice. My close friends, who always bring a smile to my face and only want the best for me, even when I'm struggling and can't see clearly. All of my loved ones that are close to me, who give me the love and support I don't quite know how to show to myself.

My Granda Alfie, who is like a best friend to me and has taught me so much over the years, especially recently. His happiness and contentment with life is something I strive for and he is the epitome of a gentleman.

Most of all, my Nanny Mamie. There are so many moving parts in my life and they have all led me here, but without my nanny none of this would be possible. She gave me the love for baking and has taught me so much. This journey began when I was knee high to a grasshopper in her kitchen and it has brought me right back to that spot. Since then, we have had a special bond. I love her dearly and would do anything for her. She pushes me to be better in so many ways, especially as a human. And this new journey has opened up so many experiences for her to enjoy. She is one of the most wonderful human beings I know and is responsible, along with all those above, for the person I am today and for whatever I go on to achieve in this wee life of mine. As long as it produces happiness, love and memories with those I care for, it will be a huge success in my eyes.

Love Jonny x

About the Author

Jonny Murphy, AKA The Hungry Hooker, is a former professional rugby player who always had a love for baking and cooking. He developed this love as a child from his Nanny Mamie. Unfortunately, he was forced to retire early from rugby due to injury and with the encouragement of those close to him started a small wholesale bakery. He is currently back home in Co. Down, Northern Ireland, reliving his childhood baking and cooking traditional homely recipes with his nanny.

LAKERS
6

Ebury Press

UK | USA | Canada | Ireland | Australia
India | New Zealand | South Africa

Ebury Press is part of the Penguin Random House group of companies whose addresses can be found at global.penguinrandomhouse.com

Penguin Random House UK
One Embassy Gardens, 8 Viaduct Gardens,
London SW11 7BW

penguin.co.uk
global.penguinrandomhouse.com

First published by Ebury Press in 2025

1

Editorial Director: Ru Merritt
Project Editor: Emily Preece-Morrison
Design: Claire Rochford
Photography: Joe Woodhouse
Food Stylist: Lou Kenney
Prop Stylist: Louie Waller

Colour origination by Altaimage Ltd
Printed and bound in Germany by Mohn Media

The authorised representative in the EEA is Penguin Random House Ireland, Morrison Chambers, 32 Nassau Street, Dublin D02 YH68.

A CIP catalogue record for this book is available from the British Library

ISBN 9781529943641

Penguin Random House is committed to a sustainable future for our business, our readers and our planet. This book is made from Forest Stewardship Council® certified paper.